Systems Safety

Including DOD Standards

Donald Layton

Weber Systems Incorporated

Systems Safety Including DOD Standards

Copyright © 1989 by Weber Systems Incorporated

Published by:

Weber Systems, Inc.
8437 Mayfield Road
Chesterland, OH 44026
(216) 729-2858

For information on translations and book distributors outside of the United States, please contact WSI at the above address.

Manufactured in the U.S.A.
ISBN: 0-938862-64-2

PREFACE

This book has been prepared as a resource document for a self-study course on system safety as it applies to activities within the United States Department of Defense (DoD). However, except for direct reference to material acquisition, formal life cycle phases and the system safety military standard, the information contained herein is applicable to any form of system safety management and engineering.

Military standard 882B, "System Safety Program Requirements" is not contained in this book, but there are enough paraphrasings and quotations included that having the MIL STD is not necessary. The user may, however, wish to obtain a current copy of the standard and the Data Item Descriptions described on page 107 through normal military distribution channels.

In addition to the system safety material, overview material is presented on human factors, testing and the interfaces between system safety and the other assurance disciplines.

A sample problem involving the system safety assessment of a small system is also offered.

Donald M. Layton
Registered Professional Engineer
(Safety Engineering)

TABLE OF CONTENTS

1

Introduction to DoD Safety

Definition of System Safety

It is sometimes easier to define what system safety is not. It is not the yellow and black striped lines and steel-toed shoes of industrial safety. It is not the accident prevention program or the accident investigation program of flight safety. It is not a statistical exercise in mishap counting. But it may include all of these functions!

The "bible" of system safety, Military Standard 882B, defines system safety as:

> The application of engineering and management principles, criteria, and techniques to optimize safety within the constraints of operational effectiveness, time, and cost throughout all phases of the system life cycle.

Note the thrust and emphasis of this definition " ... within the constraints of operational effectiveness, time and cost ... ." This is not safety at any cost, but safety within the constraints of the real world. This reflects where we are today. The old school attitude was, "If it might cause the loss of a life or the loss of a weapon system, then terminate the function." But the current attitude is,

"If this function is necessary for mission accomplishment, then everyone, not only the safety types, must set about to find the best -- and safest -- way to perform the function."

Note also that the MIL STD refers to *all* phases of the system life cycle. Although there has always been some consideration of safety in the new design/new procurement process, the principal emphasis has been on the operational phase of the life cycle. This is the "band-aid" approach -- "Fly it -Break it - Fix it - and Fly it again."

This is not only unsatisfactory from the operational viewpoint, because of weapon systems and people out of service, but it is *very* ineffective from a cost standpoint. The cost of re-design and retrofit is always considerably more than if safety had been properly designed into the system at the outset (figure 1.1).

And one must also include, in the ultimate cost of redesigning, the negative utility of the resources that have already been expended on the unsafe system.

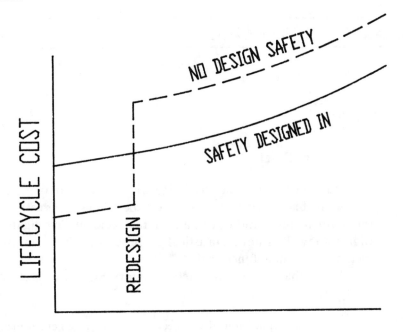

Figure 1.1. Cost of safety

History of DoD System Safety

One of the first public utterances on behalf of system safety occurred when Mr. Bill Steiglitz of Fairchild Aviation presented a paper to the Institute of Aeronautical Science in September 1947, in which he stated:

"Safety must be designed and built into airplanes, just as are performance, stability and structural integrity. A safety group must be just as important a part of the manufacturer's organization as a stress, aerodynamics or a weights group."

Not until the early 1960's, however, was the formal system safety concept applied to contractual directions. This began to replace the familiar practice in which each designer, manager and/or engineer presumably independently assumed his own share of the responsibility for safety. System safety techniques and procedures grew with the introduction of published exhibits, specifications and standards.

In April 1962 the Ballistics System Division of the U. S. Air Force Systems Command produced their Exhibit 62-41, "System Safety Engineering for the Development of Air Force Ballistic Missiles." This document established system safety requirements for the associate contractors on the Minuteman Missile. This was the first formal military system safety effort, which came about from a demonstrated need to improve the safety of this weapon system.

In September 1963, the U. S. Air Force and the U. S. Navy issued similar military specifications titled, "General Requirements for Safety Engineering of Systems and Associated Subsystems and Equipment." These two specifications were later joined into a joint military specification, MIL-S-38130 (ASG). While this activity was going on, the U.S. Army developed its own system safety specification and incorporated it into the contract for the Lockheed Cheyenne rigid rotor helicopter.

In June 1966 the joint specification became Department of Defense (DoD) requirement MIL-S-38130A.

This specification was later revised and changed into a military standard, MIL STD 882, which was expanded and revised into MIL STD 882A in June 1977. Emphasis was placed on the MIL STD in December 1978 by DoD Instruction 5000.36, "System Safety Engineering and Management," which stated:

> "The Heads of DoD components shall establish System Safety programs and apply MIL STD 882A ... for each *major* system acquisition .... Military Standard 882A shall also be applied in the acquisition of other systems and facilities, as appropriate, based on the *severity* of associated hazards and the *potential* for loss or damage."

In March 1984, MIL STD 882A was changed into a "task" format similar to that used in other "ility" disciplines, such as reliability, and renumbered as MIL STD 882B. This format placed each management and engineering activity, or task, in a separately numbered paragraph so that the managing activity (MA) can selectively invoke desired tasks to fit the requirements of the project.

Military Standard 882B

The purpose of the standard, as stated in MIL STD 882B is:

> "To provide uniform requirements for developing and implementing a system safety program of sufficient comprehensiveness to identify the hazards of a system and to impose design requirements and management controls to prevent mishaps by eliminating hazards or reducing the associated risk to a level acceptable to the managing activity (MA)."

The term *managing activity* usually refers to the Government procuring activity, but may include prime or associate contractors or subcontractors who wish to impose safety tasks on their suppliers.

Definitions

Definitions applicable to system safety are to be found in MIL STD 882B, and Army Regulation 385-16. Only a few will be repeated here for emphasis.

Accident	An unplanned event or series of events that result in death, injury, or illness to personnel or damage to or loss of equipment or property. (An accident is called a *mishap* in MIL STD 882B.)
Hazard	A condition that is prerequisite to a mishap.
Hazard probability	The aggregate probability of occurrence of individual hazardous events.
Hazard severity	An assessment of the worst credible mishap that could be caused by a specific hazard.
Risk	An expression of the possibility of a mishap in terms of hazard severity and hazard probability.
Safety	Freedom from those conditions that can cause death, injury, occupational illness or damage to or loss of equipment or property.
System safety program	The combined tasks and activities of system safety management and system safety engineering that enhance operational effectiveness by satisfying the system safety requirements in a timely, cost-effective manner throughout all phases of the system life cycle.

System Safety Program Objectives

The objectives of a system safety program are:

1. To design safety, consistent with mission requirements, into the system in a timely, cost effective manner.
2. To identify, evaluate and eliminate the hazards associated with each system (or reduce the risks of these hazards to a level acceptable to the MA0 throughout the entire life cycle of a system.)
3. To consider and use historical safety data, including lessons learned from other systems.
4. To seek minimum risk in accepting and using new designs, materials, and production and test techniques.
5. To take actions to eliminate hazards or reduce risks to a level acceptable to the managing activity (MA).
6. To minimize retrofit actions required to improve safety through the timely inclusion of safety features during research and development and system acquisition.
7. To accomplish changes in design, configuration, or mission requirements in such a manner that a risk level acceptable to the managing activity is maintained.
8. To give consideration to safety and ease of disposal and demilitarization of any hazardous materials associated with the system.
9. To document significant safety data as "lessons learned" and to submit these data to data banks or as proposed changes to applicable design handbooks and specifications.
10. To document risk acceptance procedures and actions.

It is essential that system safety be introduced into the program for the development and procurement of a weapon system as early as possible. This means that system safety requirements must be included in the *statement of work* (SOW), in the *request for proposal* (RFP), and other contractual documents. The safety program should be designed at its onset so as to facilitate the continuance of the program throughout the life cycle.

The system safety program should require that system safety be an essential part of program management. For instance, system safety engineering management analysis should be incorporated as a specific process leading to comprehensive design hazard identification, including a closed-loop system for timely action on identified hazards. In addition, system safety must be a requisite element of system testing and verification, and system safety criteria and information must be developed within the program organization.

System Safety Program Plan

The system safety program plan (SSPP) is the *contractor's* statement as to how he intends to implement the safety tasks specified by the statement of work. These tasks should require that the contractor perform and report hazard analyses; give specific direction to the subcontractor's safety efforts; and prepare documentation and reports in support of the system safety effort.

System Safety Management Plan

The system safety management plan (SSMP) is prepared by the *managing activity* in a format similar to the following:

1. General purpose requirements
2. Tasks (including action agency)
3. Organization of the Program Management Office
4. Milestones
5. Risk management (identification procedures and decision authority).
6. Administration (system safety working group, hazard tracking and distribution of deliverable data)
7. Resources (budget, manpower, authority)

The System Safety Process

The system safety process is a logical, engineered approach which intends to meet the system safety objectives.

The steps in the system safety process are as shown in figure 1.2.

Lessons Learned

The system safety process commences with a review of the lessons learned from previous systems. Unfortunately, in the past safety records were fragmented and difficult to collate.

Although accident records for military aircraft were well maintained, similar data regarding hazardous occurrences that had been successfully solved were not as readily available. This material was usually found only in the contractor's private files and a few other scattered sources.

Because these data are essential to a new design, one of the principal facets of MIL STD 882 series has been the collection of hazard analysis data from contractors so that this information can be placed in archival files for future retrieval and use.

System Specifications

To assure optimum safety, one must know the full extent of the system, as well as the specifications that define its limits and operational requirements. For example, one must consider whether maintenance is a part of the system, and how often men interact with machines.

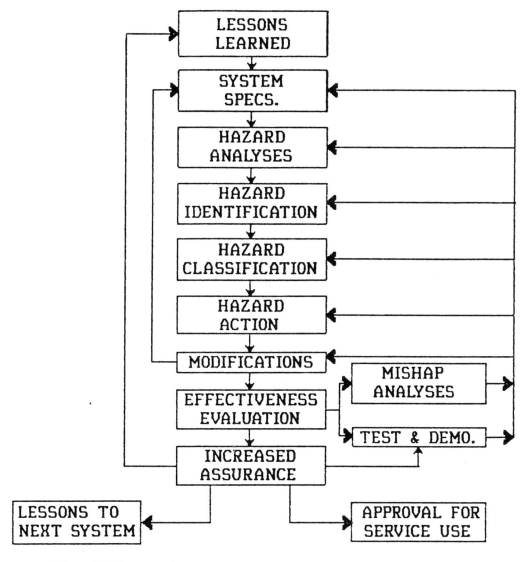

Figure 1.2. System safety process

System Hazard Analysis

Hazard analysis is the identification and evaluation of hazards, coupled with the development of recommendations for the elimination or control of the hazards. MIL STD 882B details four types of hazard analysis, which will be discussed later.

Hazard Identification

Determining what constitutes a hazard ranges from simple matters for obvious problems to complicated abstracts for new systems, processes or materials. A hazard must be identified before it can be controlled, and unfortunately, sometimes a hazard must produce a mishap before it is recognized as such.

Hazard Categorization and Evaluation

It is difficult, if not impossible, to eliminate every hazard. Therefore, it is necessary to evaluate hazards, usually on the basis of the damage they may cause (hazard severity) and the likelihood of their occurrence (hazard probability). The process of hazard evaluation and ranking is termed *risk management*.

Actions to Eliminate or Control Hazards

The purpose of hazard identification and hazard analysis is not just scorekeeping. The purpose of collecting this information is to take some action to eliminate or control the hazard. The development of proper hazard elimination actions is perhaps the most crucial element in the entire process.

Modification of System Elements

The actions taken usually result in the modification of one or more of the elements of the system. These actions are not limited to changes in the hardware or software. Procedures may also have to be changed to eliminate or control the hazards.

When a change is to be made, just as one considered the specifications and requirements in the original design, one must reconsider them in any re-design.

Effectiveness Evaluation of Action Taken

One must do more than just decide to take a corrective action. One must consider whether or not the action is cost effective and mission effective. There are two principal ways to evaluate the effectiveness of a solution: mishap analysis and testing and demonstration.

Mishap Analysis

If a course of action was adopted which results in a mishap, the action taken was incorrect. Though a basic method of system safety is to avoid using accidents as guides for safety improvement, if failure does occur because of some modification, the failure must be used to inspire a safer procedure.

Test and Demonstration

A less traumatic method of evaluating the effectiveness of a safety modification is through the process of test and evaluation. One must make certain, of course, that he is testing or demonstrating the proper items for the proper purpose. One should also be cognizant of any additional safety lessons that might be learned while testing for some other safety problem.

The results of both mishap analysis and test and evaluation are fed back into the system safety process to ascertain if there are specification conflicts, if any new safety problems have developed, and/or if there is any safety interface with other systems. These results should also be used to validate the information that made up the "lessons learned" step which began this entire process.

Increased Safety Assurance

By proceeding through the safety process, one develops an increased assurance as to the safety of the product. This provides some degree of confidence as the system is approved for final test or for production.

Documenting the Lessons Learned

The final step in the system safety process is documenting the lessons learned in a form so that they will be available for consideration for future systems.

It is to be seen that, except for additional new terms such as "hazard analysis," the system safety process is a variation of "the scientific method," which is, in fact, a logical sequencing of considerations.

Cost of Safety: Value of Safety

The cost of safety is the total expenditure of resources allocated to the safety effort. This is usually not too difficult to compute, one of the few problems being the removal of proposed modifications which received safety tags in order to boost their priority in funds allocation, but which were really not safety matters.

Though the cost of safety is usually identified and frequently highly visible, the value of safety, on the other hand, is an intangible that is very difficult to define except in retrospect. Even if a mishap resulting in the loss of a system could have been prevented through some corrective action, who can say with a high degree of certainty that, without this corrective action the mishap might not have occurred anyway?

This is a problem that constantly besets system safety practitioners. The reliability section can state, after testing, "We find that, over the long run, this bolt will break once in every hundred thousand uses." The system safety people can then say only, "When that bolt breaks, there *may* be an accident."

The value of safety can usually be definitive only after a mishap. Then one can say, with some degree of authority, "If this safety action had been applied, that mishap could have been avoided."

Summary

The benefits of a system safety program include:

1. The early identification of safety design and performance requirements.
2. The feedback of "lessons learned" from previous systems into the system being developed.
3. The early identification and evaluation of hazards inherent in a system design, thus minimizing the impact of design changes.
4. The definition of those actions necessary to minimize the effects of those hazards which cannot be totally eliminated or controlled.

Self-Study Questions

1. The military document approved by DoD for all DoD departments and agencies to use in developing system safety programs is:
   _____ a. MIL-SPEC-0001
   _____ b. MIL-STD 882
   _____ c. OSHA Handbook
   _____ d. MIL-F-8785

2. *Hazard severity* might well be renamed as:
   _____ a. Mishap severity
   _____ b. Probability of severity
   _____ c. Risk severity
   _____ d. Mishap probability

3. System safety:
   _____ a. Provides for early identification of safety design
   _____ b. Insures feedback of lessons learned information
   _____ c. Allows early identification and evaluation of hazards
   _____ d. All of the above

4. Prior to the system safety concept, the principal emphasis on safety was generally in the:
   _____ a. Concept phase
   _____ b. Demonstration/validation phase
   _____ c. Full-scale development phase
   _____ d. Deployment (operational) phase

5. The most effective safety program is safety at any cost.
   _____ a. True
   _____ b. False

6. Hazard problems and successful solutions from other similar systems are brought into the system safety process during:

_____ a. Hazard identification

_____ b. Hazard action

_____ c. Lessons learned

_____ d. Effectiveness evaluation

7. The earliest that system safety can be brought into a new program is:

_____ a. During critical design review

_____ b. As an engineering change proposal

_____ c. In the demonstration/validation phase

_____ d. In the statement of work and/or request for proposal

8. The basic concept of system safety is the elimination of all identified hazards.

_____ a. True

_____ b. False

9. Which of the following activities are not normally a part of the system safety process?

_____ a. Application of lessons learned

_____ b. System hazard analyses

_____ c. Request for proposal

_____ d. Review of system specifications

10. System test and evaluation is entirely separate from system safety:

_____ a. True

_____ b. False

11. The term *risk* has to do only with:

_____ a. The dollar cost of a mishap

_____ b. The likelihood of personal injury

_____ c. The damage to a system

_____ d. The effects of both hazard probability and hazard severity

12. The term *managing acitivy* usually refers to:

_____ a. The government procuring activity

_____ b. The Navy

_____ c. The prime contractor

_____ d. The Department of Defense

13. Hazard probability is:
_____ a. A condition prerequisite to a mishap
_____ b. An assessment of the worst credible mishap that could occur
_____ c. The relationship between hazard likelihood and severity
_____ d. An unplanned event that results in injury or damage

14. Safety is defined as the freedom from those conditions that can cause:
_____ a. Death or personal injury
_____ b. Occupational illness
_____ c. Damage to or loss of property
_____ d. All of the above

15. One of the benefits of a system safety program is the ability to point out those hazards that cannot be eliminated so that their effects may be minimized.
_____ a. True
_____ b. False

2

Language of System Safety

Definitions - General

Safety

Different people have different interpretations of just what safety is. For example, Webster's dictionary defines safety as "the condition of being safe; ... freedom from harm." Willie Hammer in his book *"Handbook of System and Product Safety"* says that safety is "the matter of relative protection from exposure to danger." The legal definition for DoD system safety practitioners is contained in MIL-STD-882B: "Freedom from those conditions that can cause death, injury, occupational illness or damage to or loss of equipment and property."

Note that the purists such as Webster define safety as the *freedom* from harm, while the practicalists such as Hammer define safety as *relative* protection. Also note that the MIL STD 882B definition indicates that no operating system can be *absolutely* safe.

Because of this, proponents of the term *risk management* say that safety is an impossible dream, and that one must concentrate on the management of the risks. A similar theme is found in the use of the term *product assurance*. This name usually encompasses more than just safety, and includes maintainability, reliability, and other criteria.

System

Funk & Wagnalls' dictionary states that a system is "an orderly combination or arrangement of parts, elements, etc., into a whole." Webster defines a system as "an aggregation or assemblage of objects united by some form of regular interaction or interdependence; a group of diverse units so combined as to form an integral whole and to function, operate or move in unison, and often, in obedience to some sort of control."

Note that words such as "orderly," "combination," "arrangement," "assemblage," "interaction," "group," "combined," "unison," and "control" emphasize *organization*. For this reason system engineering brings the various parts of different entities into a harmonious whole. Organization is the keynote of system engineering. No one has the expertise to do all the jobs alone.

System safety, therefore, becomes the organized safety of the entire system. A system safety engineer's role is to integrate the safety aspects of the design, engineering, production and use of the system.

Other Definitions (From MIL STD 882B and Army Regulation 385-16)

Items shown with a page number reference were taken from AR 385-16, while items with a paragraph number were taken from MIL STD 882B.

Accident	[p. 11] An unplanned event or series of events that result in death, injury or illness to personnel, or damage to or loss of equipment or property.
Hazard	[3.1.3] [p. 11] A condition that is prerequisite to a mishap.
Hazardous event	[3.1.4] An occurrence that creates a hazard.
Hazardous event probability	[3.1.5] The likelihood, expressed in qualitative or quantitative terms, that a hazardous event will occur.
Hazard probability	[3.1.6] The aggregate probability of occurrence of individual hazardous events that create a specific hazard.
Hazard severity	[3.1.7] An assessment of the worst credible mishap that could be caused by a specific hazard.

Mishap	[3.1.9] An unplanned event or series of events that result in death, injury, occupational illness or damage to or loss of equipment or property. (This is the MIL STD definition of an accident.)
Residual hazards	[p. 12] Hazards that are not eliminated by design.
Risk	[p. 12] An expression of possible loss in terms of hazard severity and hazard probability.
Risk	[3.1.11] An expression of the possibility of a mishap in terms of hazard severity and hazard probability.
Safety	[3.1.12][p. 12] Freedom from those conditions that can cause death, injury, occupational illness or damage to or loss of equipment or property.
System safety	[3.1.15] [p. 12] The application of engineering and management principles, criteria, and techniques to optimize safety within the constraints of operational effectiveness, time, and cost throughout all phases of the system or facility life cycle.
System safety lessons learned	[p. 12] A collection of real or potential safety or health-related problems based on data analysis or experience that can be applied to future and current systems to prevent similar recurrences.
System safety program	[3.1.21] The combined tasks and activities of system safety management and system safety engineering that enhance operational effectiveness by satisfying the system safety requirements in a timely, cost-effective manner throughout all phases of the system life cycle.
System safety program plan	[p. 12] A description of planned methods to be used by the contractor to implement the tailored requirements of this standard, including organizational responsibilities, resources, method of accomplishment, mile-

stones, depth of effort, and integration with other program engineering and management activities and related systems.

System safety program plan   [3.1.22] A formal document that fully describes the planned safety tasks required to meet the systems safety requirements, including organizational responsibilities, methods of accomplishment, milestones, depth of effort, and integration with other program engineering and management activities and related systems.

Acronyms Used in DoD System Safety

The following is a partial list of acronymns referring to DoD system safety. Those that are specifically related to the U. S. Navy are marked [N] and those that are specifically related to the U. S. Army are marked (A).

ACAT	Acquisition category
ASPR	Armed services procurement regulations
ASU	Approval for service use
BIS	Board of Inspection and Survey (Aircraft) [N]
CDR	Critical design review
CDRL	Contract data requirements list
CFE	Contractor furnished equipment
CPE	Contractor performance evaluation
DA	Developmental authority
DAL	Data acquisition list
DCP	Decision coordinating paper [N]
DHA	Design hazard analysis[N]
DID	Data item description
DP	Development proposal [N]
DSARC	Defense System Acquisition Review Council
DT	Developmental test (A)
DT&E	Developmental test and evaluation [N]
ECP	Engineering change proposal
EED	Electro-explosive device
EIR	Equipment improvement recommendation (A)
ESRB	Explosive Safety Review Board (A)
FHA	Fault hazard analysis
FMEA	Failure, mode and effect analysis
FMECA	Failure, mode, effect and criticality analysis
FOT&E	Follow-on test and evaluation [N]
FSD	Full-scale development
FTA	Fault tree analysis

GFE	Government furnished equipment
GFP	Government furnished product
HERO	Hazards of electromagnetic radiation to ordnance
HHA	Health hazard assessment (A)
IDR	Intermediate design review
ILS	Integrated logistics support
INSURV	Board of Inspection and Survey (Ships) [N]
IOT&E	Initial operational test and evaluation [N]
IPR	In-progress review (A)
JMRB	Joint Management Review Board
JMSNS	Justification, Major Starts - New System
LRU	Line replaceable unit
MADP	Material acquisition decision process (A)
MENS	Mission element needs statement
NDCP	Navy decision coordinating paper [N]
NDI	Non-development item
NEPA	National Environmental Policy Act
NPE	Navy preliminary evaluation [N]
NTE	Navy technical evaluation [N]
O&SHA	Operational and support hazard analysis
OHA	Operations (and support) hazard analysis
OPEVAL	Operational evaluation [N]
OR	Operational Requirement [N]
OSHA	Occupational Safety and Health Act
OT	Operational test (A)
OT&E	Operational test and evaluation [N]
OTEA	Operational Test and Evaluation Agency (A)
PAT&E	Production acceptance test and evaluation [N]
PDR	Preliminary design review
PHA	Preliminary hazard analysis
PHST	Packaging, handling, storage and transportation
PIP	Product improvement program (proposal) (A)
PM	Program memorandum [N]
PMO	Project management organization [N]
PMP	Program (project) master plan [N]
PR	Program (project) requirements [N]
PV	Performance verification
QA	Quality assurance
RADHAZ	Radiation hazards
RFP	Request for proposal
RFQ	Request for quotation
SAR	Safety assessment report (A)
SCA	Sneak circuit analysis
SOW	Statement of work

SSA	Source Selection Authority
SSAC	Source Selection Advisory Council
SSEB	Source Selection Evaluation Board
SSHA	SubSystem hazard analysis
SSP	System safety program
SSPP	System safety program plan
SSWG	System safety work group

Self-Study Questions

1. The system safety program plan is prepared by:
    - _____ a. The contractor
    - _____ b. The managing activity
    - _____ c. The program manager
    - _____ d. The material developer

2. System safety is applied during:
    - _____ a. Conceptual phase only
    - _____ b. Full-scale engineering phase only
    - _____ c. During production only
    - _____ d. During all life cycle phases

3. Hazards that are not removed during the design process:
    - _____ a. Are removed by the system operators
    - _____ b. Are called residual hazards
    - _____ c. Are never eliminated
    - _____ d. Are eliminated later

4. The combined tasks of safety management and safety engineering that enhance the safety of a system are called:
    - _____ a. Lessons learned
    - _____ b. Hazardous event
    - _____ c. System safety program
    - _____ d. Quality assurance

5. The abbreviation CDRL stands for:
    - _____ a. Critical design review list
    - _____ b. Contract data requirements list
    - _____ c. Contractor developed risk line
    - _____ d. Council of Defense review of logistics

6. System safety is concerned only with the improvement of the system and is not concerned with operational effectiveness.
    - _____ a. True
    - _____ b. False

7. A system safety program plan:
   _____ a. Is a formal document
   _____ b. Lists contractor organizational responsibilities
   _____ c. Describes milestones and depth of effort
   _____ d. All of the above

8. Lessons learned are not limited to actual occurrences.
   _____ a. True
   _____ b. False

9. MIL STD 882B defines *risk* as:
   _____ a. The possibility of mishap
   _____ b. The severity of a hazard
   _____ c. The probability of a hazard
   _____ d. Potential cost of a mishap

10. O&SHA stands for:
    _____ a. Operational and support hazard analysis
    _____ b. Ordnance safety hazard analysis
    _____ c. Occupational safety and Health Act
    _____ d. Organizational safety and health analysis

11. A *system* is:
    _____ a. An orderly combination or arrangement of parts
    _____ b. A part of a weapon support equipment
    _____ c. Hardware only
    _____ d. Software only

12. Hazard severity is an assessment based on the average damage or injury that would occur.
    _____ a. True
    _____ b. False

13. System safety is concerned with:
    _____ a. Management practices
    _____ b. Engineering practices
    _____ c. Safety optimization
    _____ d. All of the above

14. Although system safety is a relative term, MIL STD 882 uses the terms:
    _____ a. Freedom from ...
    _____ b. Relative freedom from ...
    _____ c. Relative protection ...
    _____ d. Complete absence of ...

15. System safety is limited to actions on hardware deficiencies.
    _____ a. True
    _____ b. False

3

Material Acquisition Cycle

Material Acquisition Decision Process

The *material acquisition decision process* (MADP) enables acquisition management decision makers to influence and approve a system acquisition process at key milestones. The process must insure the most practicable method of correcting a deficiency or responding to a threat while using current technical and manufacturing capabilities, considering limited resources, affordability and supportability. The decision process is conducted by a series of MADP reviews at predetermined milestones in the acquisition process throughout the life cycle of the system.

The Life Cycle Process

The *life cycle process* defines the progressive development of a system from its conception through its disposal. In general, this process applies to all systems, no matter what size, but the process has special meaning for major systems because of statutory requirements of life cycle phases.

The names of these phases may change, but the process is nearly always the same. These phases are:

1. Concept exploration/programming and requirements development phase (conceptual or concept phase).
2. Demonstration and validation design phase(definition or contract definition phase).
3. Full-scale development/final design phase(engineering development, and, if applicable, prototype development).
4. Production phase.
5. Deployment (use) phase.
6. Disposal phase.

General Procurement Cycle

Conceptual Phase

For programs exceeding established DoD dollar criteria, a *justification for major system, new starts* (JMSNS) is prepared by the combat developer (together with the material developer and the logistician) and is approved by the Secretary of Defense. For all other programs, the approval of an *operational and organizational* (O & O) plan constitutes an agreement between the combat developer and the material developer that a mission deficiency exists.

The JMSNS describes the operational requirements for the proposed new system as a concise expression of operational needs, operational concepts, performance goals, reliability, maintainability, and safety.

The conceptual phase has several objectives. One is the development of a technically feasible, logistically supportable and cost-effective design concept to satisfy the operational concept for the new system. Another objective is the development of the acquisition plan, technical data base, and documentation of contract requirements for the next (validation) phase. The transformation of conceptual alternatives into system design criteria is yet another goal. The final objective is the prevention of prematurely initiating an acquisition system for which the technical problems and associated risks have not been identified, investigated, or clearly documented.

The end of the conceptual phase is the preparation of the documentation for the *Joint Requirements and Management Board* (JRMB), formerly called the *Defense System Acquisition Review Council* (DSARC).

Validation Phase

In the validation phase, design information from the conceptual phase is converted into hardware design criteria suitable for further development. Design drawings are commenced and specifications for major subsystems and equipment are developed.

The concepts previously derived are now checked for technical feasibility, logistic supportability and cost-effectiveness. Functional requirements are allocated to the lower level components so that when they are integrated into the system they will satisfy the requirements of the specifications.

Entry of the validation phase is called *milestone I*. These are the criteria for entry:

(a)   Approval of a *system concept paper* (SCP) describing the acquisition strategy for the rest of the program;

(b)   Completion of the *concept formulation package* (CFP);

(c)   Estimation of cost and schedule, i.e., design to cost (DTC) goals;

(d)   Approval of the *test and evaluation master plan* (TEMP);

(e)   Identification of system safety and health issues.

The objectives of the *validation phase* include the development of the detailed hardware design for the system and verification of its operational effectiveness, supportability and lifecycle costs; the development of a technical data base and contract documentation package for the full-scale development phase; and the refinement of critical test and evaluation issues.

The result of the validation phase is the preparation of the documentation package for the JMRB II.

Full-Scale Development Phase

In the *full-scale development phase,* detailed production designs are prepared and proofed.

The criteria for entry into the full-scale development phase (Milestone II) include:

(a)   Preparation of the *decision coordinating paper* (DCP) with an updated *acquisition strategy* (AS);

(b)   Preparation of the *integrated program summary* (IPS);

(c)   Preparation of statements about manning and training such as the *required operational capability* (ROC) and *military occupational speciality* (MOS) decisions;

(d)   Identification of resources for training devices, prototypes for development testing and operational testing;

(e)   Establishment of *design to cost* (DTC) goals and *design to unit production cost* (DTUPC) goals;

(f)   Approval of *integrated logistic support* (ILS) plan;

(g)   Completion of system safety and health hazards assessment.

The objectives of the full-scale development phase include:

(a)   Transformation of validated design into full scale production designs;

(b)   Confirmation of the operational suitability of the system;

(c)   Determination that the system can be operated and maintained by personnel with skill levels anticipated to be available under service conditions, with the anticipated logistic support.

The result of the full-scale development phase is the preparation of the documentation package for the JMRB III.

Production/Deployment Phase

JMRB III (or its equivalent for minor programs) leads to the decision for production/deployment. The system is then produced in accordance with the approved design decisions and, after post-production tests, is deployed for use by the operational forces.

The criteria for entry into the *production and deployment phase* (milestone III) include:

(a) Completion of adequate developmental test and operational test reports and independent evaluations;

(b) Determination that the system is suitable and qualified for the intended mission;

(c) Approval of the integrated logistics plan by the material developer;

(d) Completion of *producibility engineering and planning* (PEP);

(e) Reevaluation of the material requirements by the compat developer;

(f) Updating of the system safety and health hazards assessments.

The prime objective of the production phase is to produce a system exactly as approved in the previous phase, with improvements and changes found necessary during the production process. Systems produced in large quantities are frequently put in "block lots" in order to maintain some form of configuration control, even though changes may be introduced during the production lifetime.

Disposal Phase

This phase is generally non-formal and consists of the removal of the system from operational use and the disposal of the system. The disposal may require removal of classified equipment, removal or modification of certain sensitive sub-systems, and proper disposal of hazardous materials.

Life Cycle Process - A Summary

The previous information is a summary of the life cycle process as it would apply to a major weapon system, and although a minor system might not require all of the formal action (such as JMRB), the cycle is similar.

Even an *engineering change proposal* (ECP) or a change order starts with an idea (concept) in which several alternatives are considered and a "best idea" is selected. This concept is then validated and developed into a full scale program that is then produced and deployed. The actions are similar, regardless of the size of the program.

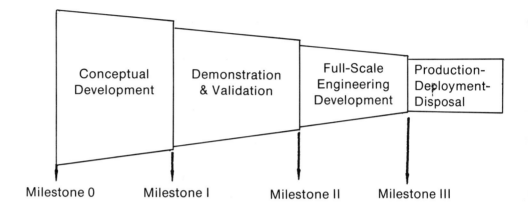

Figure 3.1. Life cycle process.

Research and Exploratory Development

Although research activity may be considered to have its own life cycle since it starts with some concept and the concept is validated and developed until the research article is engineered, produced and used, this activity is outside the normal life cycle activity. At times, when the exploratory development comes to fruition, the system undergoing research may suddenly be thrust into full production without the checks and balances in systems following the conventional life cycle process.

Non-Developmental Items

It is becoming more and more common for the military services to purchase off-the-shelf hardware. Unfortunately, these systems are frequently not subjected to the close scrutiny usually given to "fully developed" systems. Even if the system has been developed under rather stringent guidelines, these guidelines may differ significantly from those of the United States Department of Defense. As an example, a civilian aircraft may have been produced under strict Federal Aviation Administration requirements, but in many cases these requirements fall short of what the Department of Defense has stipulated as the minimum for DoD aircraft.

Self-Study Questions

1. Which of the following is *not* one of the life cycle phases?
   _____ a. Conceptual development
   _____ b. Disposal
   _____ c. Demonstration
   _____ d. Hazard analysis

2. The objective of the validation phase is:
   _____ a. Transformation of concepts into production designs
   _____ b. Verification of the adequacy of the detailed hardware design
   _____ c. Inspection and testing of systems and sub-systems
   _____ d. Identification of critical parts and assemblies

3. During what life cycle phase is it determined that the system under development can be operated and maintained with the skill levels of the anticipated user?
   _____ a. Demonstration/validation
   _____ b. Full-scale engineering
   _____ c. Conceptual/developmental
   _____ d. Production/deployment

4. Estimates for the design-to-cost goals are established during:
   _____ a. Production phase
   _____ b. Full-scale engineering
   _____ c. Validation
   _____ d. Demonstration

5. The Justification for Major System, New Starts describes in detail the weapon system to be developed.
   _____ a. True
   _____ b. False

6. Milestone III signifies the entry into:
   _____ a. Validation/demonstration phase
   _____ b. Full-scale engineering phase
   _____ c. Conceptual phase
   _____ d. Production phase

7. Approval of the test and evaluation master plan (TEMP) usually occurs during:
   _____ a. The demonstration phase
   _____ b. The full-scale engineering phase
   _____ c. The production/deployment phase
   _____ d. The conceptual phase

8. Commencement of the conceptual phase is called:
   _____ a.   Milestone I
   _____ b.   Milestone II
   _____ c.   Milestone 0
   _____ d.   Milestone III

9. The approval of the integrated logistics plan (ILS) is a requirement for entry into:
   _____ a.   The demonstration phase
   _____ b.   The full-scale engineering phase
   _____ c.   The production/deployment phase
   _____ d.   The conceptual phase

10. The disposal phase is usually non-formal in nature.
    _____ a.   True
    _____ b.   False

11. For major systems, the decision to progress from life cycle phase to life cycle phase is made by:
    _____ a.   The program manager
    _____ b.   The managing activity
    _____ c.   The combat developer
    _____ d.   The Joint Requirements and Management Board

12. Confirmation of the operational suitability of a system is an objective of:
    _____ a.   The demonstration phase
    _____ b.   The full-scale engineering phase
    _____ c.   The production/deployment phase
    _____ d.   The conceptual phase

13. Life cycle phases are limited to the development of major systems.
    _____ a.   True
    _____ b.   False

14. Operational needs, operational concepts and performance goals are described in the JMSNS.
    _____ a.   True
    _____ b.   False

15. In the conceptual phase it is customary to consider only one alternative.
    _____ a.   True
    _____ b.   False

4

Safety in the Life Cycle

Introduction

The life cycle activity of material acquisition has been discussed. Now consider again the life cycle process, this time looking specifically at the role of system safety, keeping in mind the roles of the participants in the acquisition cycle.

System Safety in the Research and Exploratory Development Phase

Because of the possibility that some new system may prove to be so valuable that it goes directly from the exploratory development to production deployment with only a quick pass through the earlier life cycle phases, it would be wrong to wait until a formal life cycle process is commenced to undertake any system safety activity.

During the development of a new technology, system safety concerns should be documented. The documentation will provide the system safety background data necessary should a decision be made to implement technology within a system development program. This is particularly true of exotic and/or radically new systems that may go almost directly from research to full-scale production.

System Safety in the Concept Phase

The system safety activities in the *concept phase* might be divided into two primary categories -- one for the system and one for the program. The safety activities for the system determine the state of the safety and the requirements for safety of the various alternatives being considered. This assessment is used -- along with many other findings -- to decide which of the alternatives will be accepted as the program system.

The safety activities for the program get the program started so that it can continue throughout the life cycle. The earlier that system safety can be inserted into the program, the easier its functions will be.

The concept phase includes the preparation of a system safety program plan describing the proposed integrated system safety effort, and the evaluation of the possibilities for failure/mishap. This evaluation is made by means of a *preliminary hazard analysis* (PHA) to identify hazards associated with each alternative concept.

The "lessons learned" from designs of similar systems are reviewed in the consideration of alternative concepts so that the system safety requirements of the new system may be defined based on past experience.

The system safety activity in this phase contributes to the data bank that will be used in determining which system will be chosen (or which part of which system will be added to another system). This requires good documentation and a summary report of the results of the system safety tasks conducted during the program initiation phase to support the decision-making process.

Demonstration and Validation/Concept Design Phase

In this phase the *system safety program plan* (SSPP) is revised or updated. Tradeoff studies are conducted to reflect the impact on system safety requirements and risk. Then system design changes are recommended, based on these studies, to make sure the optimum degree of safety is achieved consistent with the performance and system requirements. The design process is a continuous series of trade-offs, and the system safety personnel must ensure that safety is not degraded by the trade-offs.

System safety requirements for system design and criteria for verifying that these requirements have been met must be established. Then preliminary hazard analyses are updated, and detailed hazard analyses are performed to determine the risk involved in system hardware and system software.

As a part of the "look ahead" to the production process, critical parts and assemblies, techniques, procedures, and requirements which may affect safety are identified to ensure that adequate safety provisions are included.

Testing and evaluation must be performed on early production hardware, especially those employing new designs, materials and/or production techniques. Analysis, inspection and test requirements for GFE or other contractor-furnished equipment must be established to verify prior to use that applicable system safety requirements are satisfied. *Operating and support hazard analyses* (O&SHA) must be performed for each test. All test plans and procedures should be reviewed and the interfaces evaluated between the test system and personnel, equipment, facilities and the test environment.

Training plans and programs for the demonstrations and a start at the plans and programs for the production article are reviewed for adequate safety considerations. This process includes system operation and maintenance, as well as logistics support.

Full-Scale Engineering Development/Final Design Phase

The requirements for this phase again include the preparation or updating of the SSPP. Preliminary engineering designs are reviewed to make certain that safety requirements are incorporated and that the hazards identified during earlier phases are eliminated, or the associated risks reduced to an acceptable level.

The *subsystem hazard analyses* (SSHA), the *system hazard analyses* (SHA) and the operating and support hazard analyses (O&SHA) are performed, and any necessary design changes are recommended. Here may be the first chance to analyze actual, specific hardware items. This may also be the first opportunity to see all of the systems so as to make full system interface analyses as well as the operating and support interfaces.

The effects of storage, shelflife, packaging, transportation, handling, tests, operation and maintenance on the safety of the system and its components are reviewed, as are effects of safety testing, and other system tests.

Engineering documentation (drawings, specifications, etc.) are reviewed to make certain that safety considerations have been incorporated and that the safety and warning devices, life-support equipment and personal protective equipment are adequate.

System safety personnel must ensure that adequate safety provisions are included in the planning and layout of the production line, in order to establish safety control of the production process so that safety achieved in design is maintained during production.

System safety personnel must participate in technical design and program reviews. Review participation is both a giving and receiving experience.

Production and Deployment Phase

The final life cycle phase at the contractor's facility begins with the production of the system and includes "roll out" and the deployment of the system to the operating forces. The system safety activity during this phase includes the identification of critical parts and assemblies, production techniques, assembly procedures, facilities, testing and inspection requirements which may affect safety. The system safety group must also see that adequate safety provisions are included in the planning and layout of the production line, and that adequate safety provisions are included in the inspections, tests, procedures and checklists for quality control of the equipment being manufactured, so that safety achieved in design is maintained during production. Quality control personnel need some hints from system safety personnel as to where to look!

System safety people must make certain that testing and evaluation are performed on early production hardware, that O&SHAs are performed for each test, and that all test plans and procedures are reviewed.

They must review technical data for warnings and cautions, and identify special procedures such as requirements in the O&SHA for safe operation, maintenance, servicing, storage, packaging, handling and transportation.

System safety people should monitor the system throughout the life cycle to determine the adequacy of the design and operating, maintenance and emergency procedures. It is to be noted that after all production has ceased, the cognizance over the weapon system may shift from the contractor to a military agency.

System Safety Programs in Other Acquisitions

There are many weapon system acquisitions that do not fit into the normal life cycle process. These include such things as facilities (construction of buildings); special projects (moving from exploratory research directly into production, as with the Sidewinder missile); and nondevelopmental items (NDI), such as purchase of off-the-shelf items from commercial sources or other governments, for use as a part of a system or a whole weapon system.

In the development of DoD facilities, special life cycle activities have been defined that accommodate the manner in which business is done in this field. As an example, the development of U. S. Army facilities under the direction of the Army Corps of Engineers has *two* concept phases: *a programming and requirement development phase* in which the installation that will use the facility does their planning and the *concept design phase,* which is an activity of the U. S. Army Corps of Engineers (USACE). There is no validation phase, as such, in Army facilities development, and the *final design phase* is akin to the full-scale engineering phase. This is followed by a *construction phase* (production) and a *use and operations phase,* which is similar to the deployment portion of the usual production/deployment phase, with the added point that the *user* has an acceptance inspection.

These specialized facility acquisition phases dictate specialized system safety activities. In a regular life cycle a major portion of the system safety analyses are focussed on the full-scale engineering phase, but in the acquisition of a facility, much of the system safety functions are in the *concept design* and in the *construction phase.* Because many of the military facilities are built to in the *construction phase.* Because many of the military facilities are built to standards rather than to detailed, original designs (wall studs are 16 inches on center, etc.), much of facility system safety has to do with interfaces and with change orders.

In order to integrate requirements into programs that do not follow the standard system life cycle phases, the MA should carefully describe what system safety data are to be submitted in the appropriate contractual documents, assuring that these data are to be submitted prior to key decision points.

System Safety in the Life Cycle -- A Summary

Although the system safety activities have been broken down into definitive life cycle blocks, the overall picture shows that most of the system safety activities are continuous throughout the cycle, as shown in figure 4.1. Examples of this are the evaluation of hazardous materials and the safety effectiveness training. In addition, although there may be legalistic boundaries to the life cycle phases (such as review board actions), the entire process is very fluid. Figures 4.2 through 4.5 show the continuity of the system safety activities throughout the life cycle. In addition, especially on large systems, the contractor may be performing some actions that fall under the full-scale engineering category even during the conceptual or validation phases.

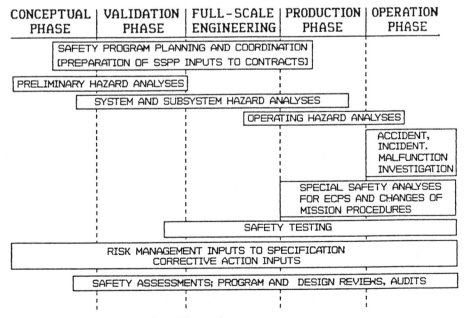

Figure 4.1. System Safety life cycle

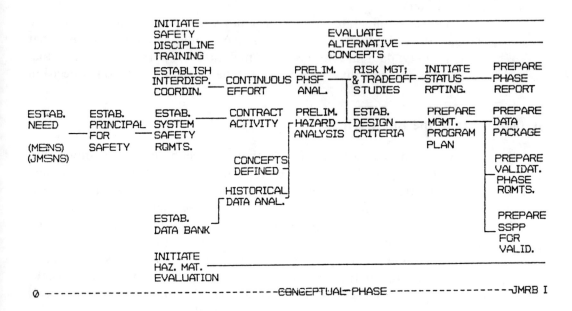

Figure 4.2. Conceptual Phase

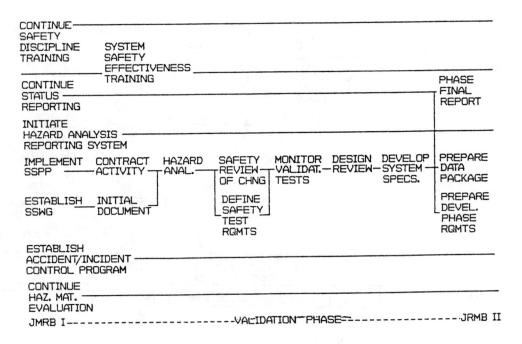

Figure 4.3. Validation Phase

34

```
CONTINUE————————————————————————————————————————————————————
SAFETY
DISCIPLINE      SYSTEM
TRAINING        SAFETY
                EFFECTIVENESS ————————————————————————————————
                TRAINING                                        PHASE
CONTINUE                                                        FINAL
STATUS ———————————————————————————————————————————————————     REPORT
REPORTING

CONTINUE
HAZARD ANALYSIS ———————————————————————————————————————————
REPORTING SYSTEM

IMPLEMENT       UPDATE      HAZARD   SAFETY    MONITOR   CRIT.      APPROVAL
SSPP     ————   PHA    ——┬— ANAL.——  REVIEW—— DEMONS. — DESIGN———— FOR FULL
                         │           OF CHNG  TESTS     REVIEW     PRODUCTION
CONTINUE_____│
SSWG

CONTINUE                 │
ACCIDENT/INCIDENT ————————
CONTROL PROGRAM                                         DEMIL./DISPOSAL
                                                        PROCEDURES  ——
CONTINUE
HAZ. MAT. ——————————————————————————————————————————————————————
EVALUATION
JMRB II --------------FULL-SCALE-DEVELOPMENT-PHASE-----------JRMB III
```

Figure 4.4. Full Scale Development Phase

```
CONTINUE————————————————————————————————————————————————————
SAFETY
DISCIPLINE      SYSTEM
TRAINING        SAFETY
                EFFECTIVENESS ————————————————————————————————
                TRAINING
CONTINUE
STATUS ———————————————————————————————————————————————————
REPORTING
                REVIEW/VALIDATE    MONITOR       MONITOR
               ┌ TEST PLANS ————— ACCEPTANCE — SURVEILLANCE ——
               │                   TESTS         TESTS
IMPLEMENT      │ CONTRACT          SAFETY REVIEW             PREPARE
SSPP     ——————┤ ACTIVITIES———————— OF CHANGES ———————————— FINAL
               │                                            PRODUCRION
CONTINUE_____│                                            PHASE RPT.
SSWG

CONTINUE
ACCIDENT/INCIDENT ——————————————————————————————————————————
CONTROL PROGRAM

CONTINUE
HAZ. MAT. ——————————————————————————————————————————————————
EVALUATION
JMRB III------------PRODUCTION/DEPLOYMENT-PHASE— — — — — — — — —
```

Figure 4.5. Production/Deployment Phase

Self-Study Questions

1. System safety activities commence after the conceptual phase.
   - _____ a. True
   - _____ b. False

2. The first preliminary hazard analyses are usually conducted during:
   - _____ a. The demonstration phase
   - _____ b. The full-scale engineering phase
   - _____ c. The production/deployment phase
   - _____ d. The conceptual phase

3. Detailed safety analyses usually can not be made until:
   - _____ a. The demonstration phase
   - _____ b. The full-scale engineering phase
   - _____ c. The production/deployment phase
   - _____ d. The conceptual phase

4. Why should system safety be considered during a research and exploratory development cycle?
   - _____ a. This phase replaces the validation phase
   - _____ b. This phase replaces the demonstration phase
   - _____ c. The system may go from R&D to production without passing through the other normal phases where system safety might bc considered.
   - _____ d. R&D is a dangerous business

5. Once safety has been established in a system, it is locked in and cannot be changed.
   - _____ a. True
   - _____ b. False

6. Operating and support hazard analyses usually are started in:
   - _____ a. The demonstration phase
   - _____ b. The full-scale engineering phase
   - _____ c. The production/deployment phase
   - _____ d. The conceptual phase

7. Hazardous materials evaluation is conducted throughout the life cycle.
   - _____ a. True
   - _____ b. False

8. The system safety program plan should be initiated during:
    _____ a.   The demonstration phase
    _____ b.   The full-scale engineering phase
    _____ c.   The production/deployment phase
    _____ d.   The conceptual phase

9. The use of system safety considerations to help determine alternative proposals is accomplished during:
    _____ a.   The demonstration phase
    _____ b.   The full-scale engineering phase
    _____ c.   The production/deployment phase
    _____ d.   The conceptual phase

10. Analysis of actual, specific hardware is usually possible for the first time on a large scale during full-scale engineering.
    _____ a.   True
    _____ b.   False

11. Facilities system safety does not follow the usual life cycle process.
    _____ a.   True
    _____ b.   False

12. The system safety activities in the conceptual phase might be divided into two primary functions, one for the system and one for:
    _____ a.   The demonstration phase
    _____ b.   The full-scale engineering phase
    _____ c.   The program
    _____ d.   Deployment

13. The primary objectives of the validation phase include:
    _____ a.   Testing of production sub-sets
    _____ b.   Evaluation of GFE
    _____ c.   Preparation of production drawings
    _____ d.   Analysis of specific hardware

14. System safety has an interest in the production line layout because:
    _____ a.   Industrial safety is a part of system safety
    _____ b.   This is a part of the O&SHA
    _____ c.   System safety usually provides production inspectors
    _____ d.   They must insure that designed in safety is built in

15. Test plans for evaluations during the validation phase must consider system safety.
    _____ a.   True
    _____ b.   False

5

Program Management

System Safety Program

The contractor is charged to establish and maintain a system safety program to support the efficient and effective achievement of overall objectives. To ensure that this is accomplished, a requirement for a system safety program must be contained in the statement of work (SOW), and Task 100 of MIL STD 882B must be imposed.

The system safety program must define a systematic approach to make certain that safety, consistent with mission requirements, is designed into the system in a timely, cost-effective manner, and that hazards associated with each system are identified, evaluated and eliminated, or the associated risk reduced to a level acceptable to the managing activity (MA) throughout the entire life cycle of a system.

To accomplish a successful safety program, the contractor must ensure that historical safety data, including lessons learned from other systems, are considered and used, and that minimum risk is sought in accepting and using new designs, materials, and production and test techniques. Actions that are taken to eliminate or mitigate the discovered risks to a level acceptable to the MA must be documented.

Through the timely inclusion of safety features during research and development and acquisition of a system, retrofit actions required to improve safety can be minimized, but necessary changes in design, configuration or mission requirements must be accomplished in a manner that does not increase the level of risk.

The design phases are the appropriate time to consider the disposal and demilitarization of any hazardous materials associated with the system.

It is essential that significant safety data be documented as "lessons learned" submitted to data banks, or as proposed changes to applicable design handbooks and specifications.

System Safety Design Requirements

In addition to the specific requirements in the standards, specifications, regulations, handbooks, etc., MIL STD 882B delineates some general system safety design requirements. These include:

- The elimination of hazards or risk reduction through design, including materal selection or substitution
- the isolation of hazardous substances, components and operations
- the location of equipment so that required access minimizes personnel exposure to hazards
- the minimization of any risk resulting from excessive environmental conditions
- the minimization of any risk created by human error in the operation and support of the system.

The designer must consider alternative approaches such as interlocks, redundancy, fail-safe design, system protection, fire suppression and protective clothing, equipment, and procedures to minimize risks from hazards that cannot be eliminated. When alternate design approaches cannot eliminate the hazard, as a last resort the designer should provide warning and caution notes in instructions and manuals, as well as distinctive markings on hazardous components and materials, equipment and facilities, to ensure personnel and equipment protection.

Not all hazards can be eliminated or mitigated, and for those residual hazards, effort should be made to minimize the severity of personnel injury or damage to equipment in the event of a mishap. Even though the improvement of inadequate safety is a continuous goal, *one must not permit overly restrictive requirements regarding safety.*

Precedence

The desired order of precedence in eliminating or mitigating hazards is as follows:

1. Design out or around the hazard.

   If at all possible, design to eliminate hazards. If an identified hazard cannot be eliminated, reduce the associated risk to an acceptable level through design selection.

2. Incorporate safety features.

   Use fixed, automatic or other protective safety design features or devices, such as interlocks and protective covers. A requirement should be established for periodic functional checks of safety devices.

3. Provide warning devices.

   When neither design nor safety devices can effectively eliminate identified hazards or adequately reduce associated risk, means shall be used to detect the condition and to alert personnel of the hazard by an adequate warning signal designed to minimize the probability of incorrect personnel reaction to the signal.

4. Use procedures, training and caution notes.

   Where it is impractical to eliminate hazards through any of the above steps, provide procedures, training and caution notes. However, without a specific waiver, no warning, caution or other form of written advisory shall be used as the only risk reduction method for category I or II hazards.

Risk Assessment

Risk assessment is based on hazard severity and hazard probability relationships. During the early design phases, the assessment is usually based on hazard severity only, since this may be all the information available. As the design proceeds and hazard probability is determined, this factor is added to the risk assessment process. Detailed discussion on the subject of risk assessment will be made in a later chapter.

Hazard Severity

MIL STD 882B provides the following definitions to be used in the classification of the severity of a mishap:

The bounds of each hazard category, such as the difference between a major system damage and a minor system damage, are stipulated by the managing activity.

In most cases the definition of the MIL STD are too broad, and additional definitions should be provided for the guidance of the contractor. For example, there should be a definitive boundary between major system damage and minor system damage. This might be expressed in terms of dollar cost, time out of service, time to repair, etc.

Table 5.1.
Hazard Severity

DESCRIPTION	CATEGORY	MISHAP DEFINITION
Catastrophic	I	Death or system loss
Critical	II	Severe injury, severe occupational illness or major system damage.
Marginal	III	Minor injury, minor occupational illness or minor system damage.
Negligible	IV	Less than minor injury, occupational illness or system damage.

Hazard Probability

Hazard probability may be either qualitative (relativistic) or quantitative (probabilistic). An example of a qualitative rating scale is that presented in MIL STD 882B:

Table 5.2
Hazard Probability

DESCRIPTION	LEVEL	SPECIFIC INDIVIDUAL ITEM	*FLEET/ INVENTORY
Frequent	A	Likely to occur frequently	Continuously experienced
Probable	B	Will occur several times in life of an item	Will occur frequently
Occasional	C	Likely to occur *some-time* in life of an item	Will occur several times
Remote	D	Unlikely but possible to occur in life of an item	Unlikely but can reasonably be expected to occur
Improbable	E	So unlikely, it can be assumed occurrence may not be experienced	Unlikely to occur but possible

* The size of the fleet or inventory should be defined.

As with hazard severity, relativistic hazard probability would also benefit from additional, amplifying definitions. It is usually necessary to stipulate just what is meant by "frequent," "several," etc. Supplemental definitions could contain such phrases as "once in every evolution," or "at least once a week."

Action on Identified Hazards

The whole point of the hazard analysis process is to take action to eliminate identified hazards or reduce the associated risk. Normally category I and II (catastrophic and critical) hazards should receive first priority for elimination or risk reduction. For some programs, such as high energy laser systems, even marginal hazards should receive high action priority. The bottom line is to identify the hazards, and then to do something about them.

Statement of Work

The following are typical statements of work for inclusion in a contract:

System Safety Program

The (weapon system, missile, avionics, etc.) contractor shall plan, implement and maintain a system safety program (SSP) which is effectively integrated into all phases of development. The provisions of MIL STD 882B shall be directly applicable except as modified herein. The primary purpose of the SSP effort shall be to identify, correct and/or control hazards during the design process within the constraints of time and system/cost effectiveness. The SSP during the contractual period shall be so established as to facilitate its continuation into later phases of the system life cycle. The SSP shall include, but not be limited to:

- System safety as an essential element of program management.

- System safety engineering analysis as a specific process leading to comprehensive design hazard identification.

- The establishment and communication of system safety criteria and information within the program organization.

- System safety as a requisite element of system testing and verification.

- Closed-loop system for action on identified hazards to ensure timely resolution.

Safety Precedence and Hazard Severity Categories

The system safety precedence of paragraph 4.4 and the hazard severity categories of paragraph 4.5.1 of MIL STD 882B shall apply.

System Safety Program Plan

The (contractor) shall prepare a *system safety program plan* (SSPP) describing in detail how he intends to conduct the safety program to comply with the requirements stated herein. The plan shall clearly delineate those tasks to be performed by subcontractors. The program plan, when approved by the procuring activity, shall be the contractual document governing the (contractor's) system safety effort.

The SSPP shall be structured in accordance with Task 101 and Data Item Description DID-SAFT-80100, and shall be arranged in the specified format. Additional sections of the SSPP may be included at the contractor's option.

The SSPP must be specific with regard to the requirements and conduct of the general unique efforts for the program requirements specified herein. Particular emphasis shall be directed toward the methods and techniques whereby the obtaining of objectives is assured by adequate management controls and coordination with other disciplines. Each task to be performed shall be independently addressed to the following extent, as a minimum:

- The (contractor's) organizational element responsible for the performance of the task, and the interrelationships and functions of the other participating organizational elements, including data typically exchanged. This requirement is also applicable to subcontractors.

- A complete description of the tasks, including the methodology for accomplishment.

- The time frame allocated for accomplishment of the tasks, including interrelationships with other program schedules and system safety tasks and report milestones.

- Documentation, including (contractor's) internal controls, data recording formats and contractually required reports.

- Resources to be allocated for the implementation of each task.

The plan shall clearly delineate those tasks to be performed by the (contractor) and those to be conducted by the subcontractors.

Self-Study Questions

1. To ensure that a system safety program is established, this requirement must be expressed in:
   - _____ a. The statement of work (SOW)
   - _____ b. MIL STD 882B
   - _____ c. The contract data requirements list (CDRL)
   - _____ d. Data item description (DID)

2. In respect to residual hazards, effort should be made to:
   - _____ a. Minimize the severity of damage
   - _____ b. Minimize the severity of injury
   - _____ c. Control mishap damage
   - _____ d. All of the above

3. Equipment should be designed so that:
   - _____ a. No access is available to hazardous materials
   - _____ b. There is minimum exposure to hazards during access
   - _____ c. Access is limited to items that can cause a mishap
   - _____ d. All hazardous materials are grouped together

4. During early design, risk assessment is based on
   - _____ a. Hazard probability only
   - _____ b. Both hazard severity and hazard probability
   - _____ c. The possible damage that could occur
   - _____ d. Hazard severity only

5. Minor injury is classified as:
   - _____ a. Catastrophic
   - _____ b. Critical
   - _____ c. Marginal
   - _____ d. Negligible

6. Complete loss of a system due to a mishap is classified as:
   - _____ a. Catastrophic
   - _____ b. Critical
   - _____ c. Marginal
   - _____ d. Negligible

7. The relativistic probability of an occurrence several times in the life of an item is classified as:
   - _____ a. Frequent
   - _____ b. Probable
   - _____ c. Occasional
   - _____ d. Remote

8. Probabilistic hazard probability is quantitative, not qualitative.

   _____ a. True

   _____ b. False

9. An occurrence several times in a complete inventory is classified relativistically as:

   _____ a. Frequent

   _____ b. Probable

   _____ c. Occasional

   _____ d. Remote

10. A system that suffers more than minor damage due to a mishap, yet is not a total loss is classified as:

   _____ a. Catastrophic

   _____ b. Critical

   _____ c. Marginal

   _____ d. Negligible

11. All hazards must be eliminated.

   _____ a. True

   _____ b. False

12. A continuously experienced happening in an inventory has the probability classification of:

   _____ a. Frequent

   _____ b. Probable

   _____ c. Occasional

   _____ d. Remote

13. If the hazard cannot be designed out, the next best thing is:

   _____ a. Providing warning devices or signals

   _____ b. Placing a note in the handbooks

   _____ c. Devising new procedures for operating

   _____ d. Installing safety features

14. It is best to consider disposal:

   _____ a. During the production phase

   _____ b. When you are ready to get rid of the system

   _____ c. As early as possible in the life cycle

   _____ d. During full-scale production

15. Hazardous sustances:

   _____ a. Must be eliminated

   _____ b. Should be isolated

   _____ c. Must be placed in the same vicinity

   _____ d. Must not be used

6

Hazard Analysis

Definition

Willie Hammer in his book *Handbook of System and Product Safety* states that hazard analysis is the investigation and evaluation of:

1. The interrelationships of primary, initiating and contributory hazards.
2. The circumstances, conditions, equipment, personnel and other factors involved in the safety of a product or safety of a system and its operation.
3. The means of avoiding or eliminating any specific hazard by the use of suitable designs, procedures, processes or materials.
4. The controls that may be required for possible hazards and the best methods for incorporating those controls in the product or system.
5. The possible damaging effects resulting from the lack of or loss of control of any hazard that cannot be avoided or eliminated.
6. The safeguards for preventing injury or damage if control of the hazard is lost.

Types of Hazards

Hazards may be categorized as *primary, initiating* and *contributing* types. The *primary* hazard is the hazard that *directly* and *immediately* causes injury, death, damage or loss of equipment, degradation of functional capabilities or loss of material. The *initiating* hazard is the hazard or event that first triggered the whole sequence of hazardous events. The *contributing* hazard is the condition that aided in the fulfillment of the undesired event.

For example, consider a high pressure air tank of low carbon steel. Moisture has caused corrosion, reducing the strength of the tank, which ruptures and fragments under pressure causing fragments to strike nearby personnel.

The hazards in this situation are:

1. *Primary* - rupture of the tank
2. *Initiating* - moisture
3. *Contributing* - corrosion, tank pressure

Frequently one of the problems in hazard analysis is the failure to determine the initiating hazard because the primary and/or contributing hazards are so obvious.

General Procedures

To perform a hazard analysis, one must first consider the system restraints, such as detailed design requirements (specifications); the expected operation of the system (mission requirements); general statutory regulations such as noise abatement (regulatory requirements), standardized procedures such as switches "up" or "forward" for *on* (good engineering practices); and lessons learned from previous mishaps and near mishaps (accident experience and failure reports).

One then looks at general and specific potential accident causal factors in the equipment (hardware and software); the area where the equipment is operated (environment); the man-in-the-loop (personnel); the proposed use of the system (mission); the techniques for using the system (procedures); and the specific nature of the system when in operation (configuration).

For each of the mishap causal factors, one must evaluate the individual hazards, such as the hazards caused by the operating environment; and the interface hazards, such as the hazards due to personnel operating in a specified environmental condition.

To evaluate the damage possibility of a hazard, one may use either a qualitative analysis, a quantitative analysis, or both. The qualitative analysis, in general, looks for possible safeguards against damage. These include alternative designs, alternative procedures, and/or damage containment. For each safeguard, one must question the system restraints on whether the proposed solutions exceed the imposed constraints.

A quantitative hazard evaluation requires the development of a mathematical model of the system. There may be a problem if all of the required data is not available. Some data can be mathematically synthesized, but other data may not be amenable to quantification. As a result, the model may have to be modified to accommodate those gaps.

From these analyses, one determines a relativistic safety level (from qualitative analysis) or a probabilistic safety level (from quantitative analysis). One then determines corrective actions, while keeping in mind procedural and operational trade-offs and cost comparisons.

General Types of Hazard Analyses

One classification of hazard analysis refers to the time in which the analysis is conducted -- before the design is made, or after the design is completed. *Predesign* analyses determine and evaluate those hazards that might be present in a system *to be* developed, while *postdesign* analyses determine whether the selected equipment and procedures meet the standards and criteria that have been established.

Unfortunately, strict procedures and criteria may not have been established prior to the design, so that in the postdesign analysis one must also look for potential hazards in a predesign analysis. No matter which type of analysis is performed, the other must be done to some extent.

Another breakdown of hazard analysis is quantitative and qualitative, as discussed in the general procedures. *Qualitative* analyses are non-mathematical reviews of all factors affecting the safety of a product, system, operation or person, while *quantitative* analyses use mathematical relationships. There is no regard for probability of occurrence of an event in a qualitative analysis. A qualitative analysis of some degree must precede a quantitative analysis.

The frequency of occurrence of a hazard in an analysis may be expressed in either a relativistic or probabilistic manner.

Relativistic refers to the rough frequency with which a specific event has occurred with existing, operational items. Each hazardous condition is rated in accordance with some predetermined listing to indicate the degree of care that must be exercised with the new system. Such a listing might be:

1. Remote - no record of past occurrence in similar systems.
2. Random - has occurred once in the history of items reviewed.
3. Seldom - has occurred two or three times.
4. Chronic - has occurred more than three times.

Numerical ratings may be assigned to scales to permit a qualitative event to be quantified. An example of this is the Cooper-Harper Scale for flight testing. (MIL-F-8785C)

Probabilistic refers to the use of a numerical probability, the expectancy that an event will occur a certain number of times per a specific number of trials -- *over the long run*. Probabilities can be determined from experience data on operations of similar systems, preliminary tests, synthesized combinations of values or extensions and combinations of all of these.

It is to be noted that safety probabilities (the probabilities of damage and/or injury) are not synonymous with the probabilities of success or failure upon which reliability is based. The expression "fail safe" is an indication that conditions and situations exist in which equipment can fail with no damage or injury occuring.

A probability guarantees nothing. It indicates only that a failure, error or mishap is deemed possible -- even though it may rarely occur -- over a period of time, or over a considerable number of operations. Unfortunately, a probability cannot indicate exactly when, during which operations, or to which person or piece of equipment a mishap will occur.

The very fact that a probability is extremely low may contribute to a hazard, if the safety of the item is not considered *because* of the low probability.

Analysis Assessment

To ensure that the hazard analyses are thorough and repeatable, it is wise to conduct some sort of assessment of the procedures. This is true for both those monitoring the action and those who are actually performing the analyses. The following is a "check-list" for assessing any type of hazard analysis:

1. Is there a "road map" to show how the analysis was done?
2. Does the bookkeeping make it easy to follow the logic used in performing the analysis?
3. Are *all* of the primary hazards listed?
4. Do the contributory hazards include all of those that have been identified in mishaps of similar systems?
5. Are the recommended hazard controls and corrective actions *detailed*?
6. Are the recommended hazard controls and corrective actions *realistic*?
7. Are the recommended actions fed back into the line management system in a positive way that can be tracked?

Products of System Safety Analyses

The following are some of the products that one might expect from a proper system safety hazard analysis:

1. Initial assessment of the significant safety problems of the program. (Have the hazards been identified?)
2. Establishment of a plan for follow-on action such as additional analyses, tests, training, etc. (Is there a strong program to do something positive?)
3. Identification of potentially hazardous equipment and personnel failure modes and improper usages. (Does the analysis lead us to what we are after -- the potential hazards?)
4. Selection of pertinent safety related criteria, requirements and/or specifications. (Have the hazards been identified with respect to documented criteria?)
5. Determination of safety factors for trade-off studies. (When trade-offs are made, is safety a strong consideration?)

6. Evaluation of hazardous designs and establishment of corrective/preventative action priorities. (Can one tell from the analysis which items need the most work?)

7. Organization of baseline data for qualitative deductive analysis. (Can one draw broad conclusions about the safety from the conclusions without a lot of digging?)

8. Identification of safety problems in subsystem environment interfaces. (What happens when we join the subsystems?)

9. Identification of factors leading to the hazardous events. (How can it all come about?)

10. Evaluation of probability of hazardous events quantitatively, and identification of critical paths of cause. (What is the chance of something happening and how *can* this occur?)

11. Description and ranking of the importance of potentially hazardous conditions. (How do we decide where to put our time and effort?)

12. Development of a basis for program-oriented precautions, personnel protection, safety devices, emergency equipment, procedures-training, and safety requirements for facilities, equipment and environment. (If one can't fix the hazard, what can be done to protect the man/machine?)

13. Provision of evidence of compliance with program safety regulations. (Did the safety group do what it was charged to do?)

Each activity may use a different form for recording the analysis of hazards. Usually the only requirement for conformity is that the contractor, the associate contractor and the subcontractors use the same form. Figure 6.1 depicts a typical form for a fault hazard analysis.

Hazard Action Report (HAR)

After the analyses have been performed and hazards identified and eliminated, controlled, or left up in the air, there must be a means to report the hazards to the managing activity, as well as to establish a record of the disposition of the hazard. The vehicle for this is the *hazard action report* (HAR). This document provides a formal proof of responsible management action in the area of safety.

All category I and II hazards identified by whatever means should be recorded on the HAR. Normally, category III and IV need not be recorded on an HAR unless specifically directed. An example of listing more than categories I and II occured in the high energy laser program, where all hazards were listed. Those hazards not listed on the HAR should be recorded elsewhere so that they are not lost. The hazard action report is normally reviewed and opened at a system safety working group (SSWG) meeting, and is closed by the acquisition manager as set forth in the system safety management plan. A "hazard index" of all "opened" HARS should be kept up-to-date.

PROGRAM	SYSTEM	REF.	PREPARED BY	REVIEWER

COMPONENT/ FUNCTION	FAULT HAZARD DESCRIPTION	HAZARD EFFECTS	PHZ	CAT	PRB	IND	(A) DETECTION (B) COR. ACTION	RECOMMENDED ACTION	REMARKS

PHAZE	CATEGORY	PROBABILITY
G - GRND T - T.O. I - INFLITE M - MAINT. L - LNDG A - ALL	MIL STD 882A	1 - FREQUENTLY 3 - OCCASIONAL 5 - IMPROBABLE 2 - REASONABLY PROBABLE 4 - REMOTE 6 - IMPOSSIBLE

Figure 6.1. Typical hazard analysis form

SYSTEM SAFETY - HAZARD ACTION REPORT (HAR)	REPORT No.	
SYSTEM	REPORTED BY PHONE	DATE
COMPONENT/SUBSYSTEM	HAZARD PROBABILITY	HAZARD CATEGORY
DRAWING No.	KEY WORDS	STATUS OPEN CLOSED
INFORMATION SOURCE	ANALYSIS	FIELD RPT.	TEST	OTHER
DESCRIPTION OF HAZARD				
RECOMMENDED ACTION				
SYSTEM SAFETY _____		PROGRAM OFFICE _____		

Figure 6.2. Typical hazard action report

The HAR identifies the hazard, probability, and criteria for control. It records the history and action of the events leading to implementation of the control and verifies that the criteria have been met. Figure 6.2 depicts a typical hazard action report form.

Hazard Analysis Types

Hazard analyses used in system safety include: (1) *preliminary hazard analysis* (PHA), which is an initial assessment of the system; (2) *subsystem hazard analysis* (SSHA), which identifies hazards in the functional relationship of the components and equipment in each subsystem; (3) *system hazard analysis* (SHA), which identifies hazards associated with subsystem interfaces; and (4) *operating & support hazard analysis* (O&SHA), which evaluates procedural safety. These analyses may be qualitative or quantitative. The managing activity may specify the format and technique to be used for hazard analyses requiring submittal or integration. The format may be a structured or unstructured narration, a matrix chart, or a logic model. Models and techniques should be compatible with those being applied by other disciplines on the same program, so that results are comparable.

In DoD system safety, the requirements for hazard analyses are included in the design and engineering tasks -- Task 2XX series of MIL STD 882B. Details of these tasks, as they relate to hazard analysis, are listed as follows.

Task 201 - Preliminary Hazard List

This task requires the contractor to examine the system concept shortly after the concept definition effort begins, and to compile a *preliminary hazard list* (PHL) identifying possible hazards that may be inherent in the design.

The PHL, with additional hazards added as they are uncovered, provides the hazards to be analyzed.

Task 202 - Preliminary Hazard Analysis

The *preliminary hazard analysis* (PHA) is the *initial* risk assessment of a concept or system. The PHA effort is normally started during the *concept exploration* phase, or the *earliest life cycle phases* to consider hazardous components; safety-related interfaces among various elements of the system; environmental constraints; operating, test, maintenance and emergency procedures; human factors engineering, facilities, and support equipment; and safety related equipment, safeguards and possible alternative approaches.

Task 203 - Subsystem Hazard Analysis

This task requires the contractor to perform and document a *subsystem hazard analysis* (SSHA) to identify all components and equipment, including software, whose performance, performance degradation, functional failure or inadverent functioning could result in a hazard, or whose design does not satisfy contractual safety requirements. This analysis should include a determination of the modes of failure, including reasonable human errors as well as single point failures, and the effect on safety when failures occur in subsystem components. The contractor should update the SSHA when needed as a result of any system design changes.

If no specific analysis techniques are directed in the contract, the contractor must obtain MA approval of technique(s) to be used, *prior* to performing the analysis.

Task 204 - System Hazard Analysis

This task requires the contractor to perform and document analyses to identify hazards and assess the risk of the *total* system, specifically of the subsystem interfaces. This analysis shall include a review of subsystem's interrelationships for possible independent, dependent and simultaneous hazardous events, including failures of safety devices and common possible hazard causes; as well as the degradation in the safety of a subsystem, or the total system, from normal operation of another subsystem; and design changes that effect subsystems.

Task 205 - Operating and Support Hazard Analysis

The *operating and support hazard analysis* (O&SHA) is designed to examine procedurally controlled activities. Here it is recognized that people are going to be involved with the system and one must account for their actions. Considered in this analysis are activities which occur under hazardous conditions, their time periods, and the actions required to minimize risk during these activities/time periods. Also considered are changes needed in functional or design requirements for system hardware/software, facilities, tooling, and support/test equipment to eliminate hazards or reduce associated risks; requirements for safety devices and equipment, warnings, cautions and special emergency procedures; requirements for handling, storage, transportation, maintenance and disposal of hazardous materials; and requirements for safety training and personnel certification.

Task 212 - Software Hazard Analysis

This task requires the contractor to perform and document software hazard analysis on safety critical software-controlled functions to identify software errors/paths which could cause unwanted hazardous conditions.

Sub-classifications of this type of analysis are the *preliminary software hazard analysis,* where software design is examined to identify unsafe inadvertent command or failure-to-command modes for resolution; and *follow-on software hazard analysis,* where software and its system interface are examined for events, faults and occurrences such as timing, which could cause or contribute to undesired events affecting safety.

Task 213 - GFE/GFP System Safety Analysis

This task requires the contractor to identify the safety critical performance and design data needed to incorporate *government furnished equipment* (GFE) and/or *government furnished products* (GFP), and to identify for the MA any additional analyses needed for interfaces between the GFE/GFP and the rest of the system.

Self-Study Questions

1. The following hazards should be identified in the Hazard Action report:
   - _____ a. Only category I
   - _____ b. Only category IV
   - _____ c. All category I and II
   - _____ d. Only residual hazards

2. The subsystem hazard analysis is concerned with:
   - _____ a. Equipment and components
   - _____ b. Interfaces
   - _____ c. Procedural matters
   - _____ d. Material furnished by subcontractors

3. Tasks to be assigned in order to ensure that hazard analyses are performed are contained in the TASK IXX series:
   - _____ a. True
   - _____ b. False

4. The system hazard analyses are concerned with:
   - _____ a. Equipment and components
   - _____ b. Interfaces
   - _____ c. Procedural matters
   - _____ d. Matters that involve a major system

5. Operating and support hazard analyses are concerned with:
   - _____ a. Equipment and components
   - _____ b. Interfaces
   - _____ c. Procedural matters
   - _____ d. Support hardware only

6. A subsystem hazard analysis may be concerned whether or not the design meets contractual safety requirements.
   - _____ a. True
   - _____ b. False

7. The products of a system safety analysis include:
   _____ a.   Plans for follow-on tests
   _____ b.   Safety factors for trade-off studies
   _____ c.   Establishment of corrective priorities
   _____ d.   All of the above

8. The hazard analysis form used during design:
   _____ a.   Must be a DoD standard
   _____ b.   Is the prerogative of the contractor and the sub-contractors
   _____ c.   Should be the same for the contractor and the sub-contractors
   _____ d.   Is stipulated by the managing activity

9. Probabilistic hazard data should only be obtained from accident statistics.
   _____ a.   True
   _____ b.   False

10. The brakes fail on a vehicle because the operator has been braking excessively. The operator loses control on the wet road and crashes. The primary cause of this mishap is:
    _____ a.   Brake failure
    _____ b.   Wet road
    _____ c.   Excessive braking
    _____ d.   All of the above

11. What is the initiating cause of this mishap?
    _____ a.   Brake failure
    _____ b.   Wet road
    _____ c.   Excessive braking
    _____ d.   All of the above

12. What is the contributory cause of this mishap?
    _____ a.   Brake failure
    _____ b.   Wet road
    _____ c.   Excessive braking
    _____ d.   All of the above

13. Hazard analysis has only to do with determining the cause of the hazard.
    _____ a.   True
    _____ b.   False

14. If a "pre-design" hazard analysis is performed, a "post-design" analysis is not required.

    _____ a. True
    _____ b. False

15. A qualitative hazard analysis:

    _____ a. Provides a numerical guarantee of hazard probability
    _____ b. Provides a numerical probability *over the short run*
    _____ c. Provides a numerical probability *over the long run*
    _____ d. Provides a relativistic probability

7

Hazard Analysis Techniques I

Introduction

Those performing hazard analyses may choose from several techniques ranging from the relatively simple to the complex. The purpose of this discussion is to present the basics of several of these techniques for general understanding, and then to concentrate on one type, the *fault tree* analysis.

Fault Hazard Analysis

The *fault hazard analysis* is an inductive method of analysis which can be used exclusively as a qualitative analysis, or, if desired, expanded to a quantitative one. The fault hazard analysis requires a detailed investigation of the subsystem to determine component hazard modes, causes of these hazards, and resultant effects to the subsystem and its operation. This type of analysis is a form of an analysis long used in reliability, called *failure mode* and *effect analysis* (FMEA), or *failure mode, effects and criticality analysis* (FMECA). The chief difference between the FMEA/FMECA and the fault hazard analysis is a matter of depth. Through the FMEA or FMECA looks at *all* failures and their effects, the fault hazard analysis is charged only with consideration of safety-related effects.

The fault hazard analysis of a subsystem is an engineering analysis to determine what can fail, how it can fail, and how frequently it will fail, as well as the effects of the failure and their importance.

A fault hazard analysis is used to aid in system design concept selection; to support "functional mechanizing" of hardware; to prompt the designer to "design around" failure modes and effects involving severe penalties; to assist in operational planning for employment of the system; and to assist management decisions with selective concentration of limited resources on "highest risk" or "highest criticality" system elements.

Only the most important modes are supposed to be considered, but it is difficult to tell which are the most important without considering all or nearly all of the modes.

The fault hazard analysis must consider both *functional modes* and *out of tolerance modes* of failure. For example, a 5%, 5K (plus or minus 250 Ohm) resistor can have *as functional failure modes, failing open or failing short* while the out of tolerance modes might include too low or too high a resistance.

To conduct a fault hazard analysis, it is necessary to know and understand the mission of the equipment, the constraints under which it must operate, and the limits delineating success and failure. The procedural steps are generally as follows:

1. The system is divided into subsystems that can be handled effectively.
2. Functional diagrams, schematics and drawings for the system and each subsystem are then reviewed to determine their interrelationships and those of the component subassemblies. This review may be done by the preparation and use of block diagrams.
3. A complete component list is prepared for each subsystem as it is to be analyzed. The specific function of each component is entered at the same time.
4. Operational and environmental stresses affecting the system are then established. These are reviewed to determine the adverse effects that they could generate on the system or its assemblies and components.
5. Significant failure mechanisms that could occur and affect components are determined from an analysis of the engineering drawings and functional diagrams. Effects of subsystem failures are then considered.
6. The failure modes of individual components that would lead to the various possible failure mechanisms of the subsystem are then identified. Basically, it is the failure of the component that produces the failure of the entire system. However, since some components may have more than one failure mode, each mode must be analyzed for its effect on the assembly and then on the subsystem. This may be accomplished by tabulating all failure modes and listing the effects of each, such as the resistors that are *open or short, high or low.*
7. All conditions affecting a component or assembly should be listed to indicate whether there are special periods of operation, stress, personnel

action or combinations of events that would increase the probabilities of failure or damage.

8. The hazard category from MIL STD 882B should be assigned.
9. Preventative or corrective measures to eliminate or control the hazard are listed.
10. Initial probability rates are entered. These are "best judgements" and will be revised as the design process goes on.
11. A preliminary criticality analysis may be done at this time.

Fault Hazard Limitations

A subsystem may have failures that do not result in mishaps, and tracking all of these down is a costly process. Even if one desired to track down all the possible failures, all failures may not be found, all failure modes may not be considered, and all failure effects may not be considered.

Analysis is usually concentrated on hardware failures, and often inadequate attention is given to human factors. For example, a switch with an extremely low failure rate may be dropped from consideration, but the wrong placement of the switch may lead to a mishap. Environmental conditions are usually considered, but the probability of occurrence of these conditions is rarely considered. This may result in "over safetying." Reliability is considered on the basis of tests, but substandard manufacture and wear are usually not considered.

One of the greatest pitfalls in fault hazard analysis (and in many other techniques, for that matter) is over-precision in mathematical analysis. Too often analysts try to obtain "exact" numbers from "inexact" data, and too much time may be spent in improving preciseness of the analysis rather than in eliminating the hazards.

Sneak Circuit Analysis

A *sneak circuit analysis* is conducted on hardware and software to identify latent (sneak) circuits and conditions that inhibit desired functions or cause undesired functions to occur *without a component having failed.* The analysis employs recognition of topographical patterns characteristic of all circuits and electrical/electronic systems.

The four basic types of sneak circuits are:
(1) Sneak *path,* which may cause current or energy to flow along an unexpected route;
(2) Sneak *timing,* which may cause current or energy to flow or to inhibit a function an at unexpected time;
(3) Sneak *condition,* which causes a false or ambiguous indication of system operating conditions; and
(4) Sneak *label,* which may cause an incorrect stimulus to be initiated.

On November 21, 1960, after more than 50 successful Redstone launches, the first Mercury-Redstone test flight was fired at Cape Canaveral. All systems were "Go" and the engine roared to life. The Redstone booster lifted off the pad for a few inches -- and then -- the engine shut down and the booster settled back down on the pad! The escape tower was ejected and the capsule parachutes were deployed.

For 28 hours the missile just sat there with no one daring to approach it until the batteries had run down and the oxygen fuel had boiled off. It was several days before the cause of the self-abort was discovered. Investigation showed that no components had "failed." The missile was still operational, but, a sneak circuit had occurred to shut off the engine.

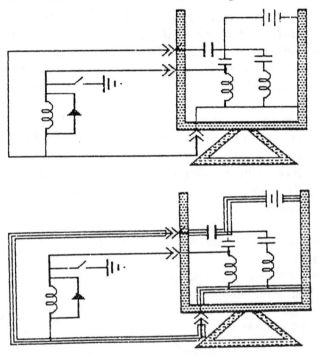

Figure 7.1. Normal circuit

In normal operations, the cutoff command relay contacts or the pad abort switch should energize the engine cutoff coil and the abort indicator coil. The launch command contacts provide power through the indicator lights (which indicate that a launch command has been given) to the ground through the tail umbilical plug.

Closing either the cutoff command contacts or the pad abort switch provides an abort signal by routing current through the abort indicator coil to the ground through the tail umbilical plug. However, if the tail umbilical is removed while the control umbilical is still attached, the launch command current follows a path through the abort indicator coil to the engine cutoff coil and to ground. And this is what happened. The tail umbilical plug had separated 29 milliseconds before the control umbilical, and in this short period, the signal had been given (and received) to shut down the missile. This was an indication of a *sneak path.*

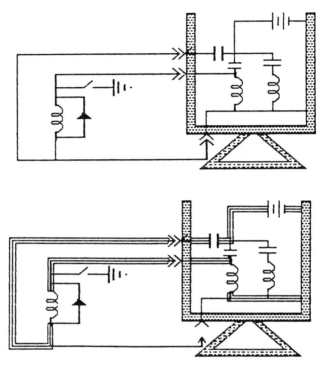

Figure 7.2. Sneak circuit

As an example of a *sneak condition,* all power is removed from a television set and the power is turned off. Therefore there is no power to the set and it is safe to work on it. *However,* there is an additional energy source that may not have been considered -- the capacitors that store a large amount of energy. And when they are grounded they discharge through the person who is working on the set!

As an example of *sneak timing,* a motor control permits the motor to run in either direction by switching the power through relays to two different (or even the same) power supplies. When relays A-010 and A-020 are closed and B-010 and B-020 are open, power flows in one direction. When the open and closed cycle of these relays is reversed, the power flows in the other direction. However, due to the nature of these relays, they can close faster than they can open. This means that for a very short period of time, both relays are closed. And the relays conduct the current from both power supplies directly to ground!

As an example of another *sneak path,* the flasher module on a car is wired directly to the battery so that the flasher can operate even with the ignition switch off (while you go for help, for example). The brake light is wired

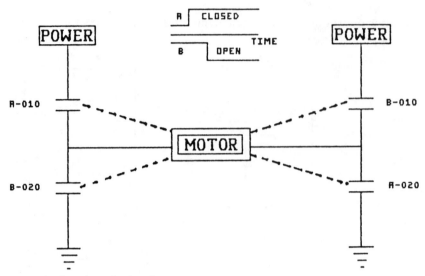

Figure 7.3. Sneak path circuit

through the ignition switch so that unless the ignition is on, pressing on the pedal will not illuminate the brake lights. The radio is also wired through the ignition switch so that when you shut off the ignition, you don't leave the radio on. You have the flasher module *on* and step on the brakes -- and the radio comes *on*!

As an example of a *sneak label*, a warning label reads *SAFE* when there is no power to the system. When the circuits are energized, a pickoff from the power energizes a solenoid to close a red-hatched cover over the word *safe*. Another pickoff from the same power source operates a *press-to-test* light. But this light draws so much current that when it is activated, the solenoid will not completely close, and thereby gives a false indication.

Data being used for sneak circuit analysis must represent the actual "as built" circuitry of the system. Functional, integrated and system level schematics do not always represent the actual constructed hardware. Detailed manufacturing and installation schematics must be used. For example, the Redstone case that was cited showed all grounds to a "Ground" without consideration of whether this was a wire, bar, case, through plugs, or what.

Complicated computer programs are used to convert circuits to node topographs, such as are shown in figure 7.4, that can be read and queried (a series of questions have been developed for each nodal form) in order to flush out the sneak condition.

A single line (no-node) topograph with a switch and a load might have clues such as:

(1) Can the switch be open if the load is desired?
(2) Can the switch be closed when the load is desired?
(3) Does the switch's label reflect the true load function?

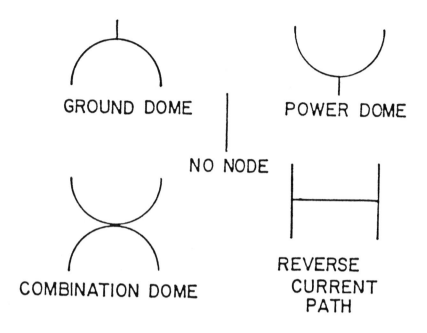

Figure 7.4. Node topographs

Energy Concept

The *energy concept* is based on the premise that all losses are caused by an interference with the normal exchange of energy. This results in the definition of an accident as an unwanted transfer of energy because of lack of barriers and/or controls, producing injury or damage to assets, preceded by sequences of planning and operational errors which failed to adjust to changes in physical or human factors and produced unsafe acts and/or unsafe conditions arising out of the risk in an activity and interrupting or degrading the activity.

Energy exposure sources can be remembered by an acronym relating to the names of the sources, METRC:

Mechanical	-	Physical events such as impact, breaking, shearing, puncturing.
Electrical	-	Events causing burns and interference with the normal electrical energy exchange.
Thermal	-	Events causing heat exhaustion, heat stroke, burns, tissue damage from freezing.
Radiant	-	(Ionizing and Non-Ionizing) Events causing cell damage.
Chemical	-	Events causing toxic exposure from inhalation, ingestion and adsorption.

The damage caused by *excessive* energy might include:

Mechanical   -   Abrasion, Erosion.

Electrical   -   Melting of motors. Thermal heat damage such as fusion of plastic.

Thermal   -   Vaporizing and deforming of assets.

Radiant   -   Creation of gas bubbles in stainless steel.

Chemical   -   Corrosion, chemical change, etc.

As an accident avoidance measure, one develops strategies for energy control similar to those listed as follows:

1. Prevent the accumulation by setting limits on noise, temperature, pressure, speed, voltage, loads, quantities of chemicals, amount of light, storage of combustibles, height of ladders, etc.

2. Prevent the release through engineering design, containment vessels, gas inerting, insulation, safety belts, lock-outs, etc.

3. Modify the release of energy by using shock absorbers, safety valves, rupture discs, blow-out panels, less incline on the ramps, etc.

4. Separate assets from energy (in either time or space) by moving people away from hot furnace, limiting the exposure time, picking up with tongs, etc.

5. Provide blocking or attenuation barriers such as eye protection, gloves, respiratory protection, sound absorption, ear protectors, welding shields, fire doors, sunglasses, machine guards, tiger cages, etc.

6. Raise the damage or injury threshold by improving the design (strength, size), immunizing against disease, warming up by exercise, getting calluses on your hands, etc.

7. Establish contingency response such as early detection of energy release, first aid, emergency showers, general disaster plans, recovery of system operation procedures, etc.

Energy Trace Analysis

An *energy trace analysis* is the input/output tracking of potentially harmful energy flows such as energy into facility, energy from facility to user, energy from user into facility, and energy from user out of facility.

The analyst must consider what would happen if energy is doing what it is *not* supposed to do, *not* doing what it is supposed to do, doing its thing too early, doing its thing too late, or doing something *where* it was not supposed to be doing it.

The procedure for an energy trace analysis requires one to select energy source groups by internal events. Such events may be electrical events (AC/DC flows); massgravity-height (mgh) events (falls and drops); rotational kinetic events (fans, machinery, etc.). Then external events such as terrestrial events (earthquake, flood, cave-in) are considered.

The starting point for each input of that type is defined, and energy flow is tracked from its starting point through the system or the subsystem branch to each transfer or use point, considering each physical and/or procedural error along the energy flow path to determine what harmful outcomes may occur when too much or too little energy flows; energy flows too soon, too late or not at all; energy flow is blocked or impeded; energy flow conflicts with another energy flow at a transfer or use point, or the barrier degrades, is disturbed or does not function at all.

The analyst assesses whether harmful outcome requires further analysis or consideration to achieve energy flow control, and if control is needed, determines the best strategy.

Simultaneous Timed Events Plotting Analysis (STEP)

The objective of a STEP analysis is to discover and/or define unsuspected, ambiguous or latent hazards or hazardous interactions associated with use. This permits the analyst to develop worksheets describing system behavior, and permits the visualizing action by a "mental movie." This enables the tracking of people and things in order to observe and define interaction problems.

The STEP analysis may find confusing, incorrect action or response triggers such as a warning light that indicates "something" wrong, rather than a definitive fault; or improperly sequenced, timed or synchronized functional interactions, such as having to open the door to an engine test cell to get the fire extinguisher. It may also detect inadequate adaptive response or reaction times or capability, and potential for bypassing equipment/operational interaction.

One can also determine from the STEP the functional capacity/-capability mismatches at interfaces (such as where an emergency shut-off valve cannot be reached from operator's station); unconventional or ambiguous task performance demands from the facility (such as where a second floor fire exit requires initially going *up* stairs); unpredictable facility or equipment interactions or behavior (such as where a room vent is located near truck parking area with its exhaust fumes); and automatic safety device subject to inappropriate human interaction in an emergency.

Management Oversight Risk Tree (MORT)

The *management oversight risk tree* is a logic tree which structures factors in an order to make clear the program or process of concern, the functions necessary to complete the program or process, and the criteria used to judge whether or not a step is done well.

MORT was originally used as an investigative tool *after* a mishap to determine what had happened in the form of oversights and ommissions, but it can be used to develop logic diagrams such as fault tree, to determine the assumed risks by listing exposures in a facility, operation or process. This latter step is a strong point for MORT since it documents these risks and makes them visible to management, particularly, those cases where the management systems are *less than adequate* (LTA). These are the occasions when planning and management systems are *not good enough* to complete the task without risks.

MORT has a three-phase approach:

1. CHANGE ANALYSIS

    This is a comparison of a mishap produced and a similar mishap-free event. The six step application in Change Analysis follows:

    a) Define the accident situation.
    b) Define a comparable accident-free situation.
    c) Compare these two situations.
    d) Set down differences.
    e) Analyze differences for their effect on an accident (or a potential accident.)
    f) Integrate the information into an accident investigation-prevention.

2. POSITIVE TREE

    This approach uses a straight-forward logic diagram to determine the state of readiness of a new facility, operation or process. The steps in this logic tree include:

    a) Structural services and hardware ready
    b) Managerial control system ready
    c) Personnel ready

3. NEGATIVE TREE

    This is constructed from the factors leading to the undesirable event, such as specific oversights and omissions, assumed risks, and Management Systems Less Than Adequate. Questions to be considered in the Negative Tree might include:

    a) Are warning signals and lights adequate and not subject to misinterpretation?
    b) Are operator and support manuals current and correct in items relating to safety?
    c) Have proper precautions been developed for the safe operation of the system?

Self-Study Questions

1. The five energy exposure sources are:
   - _____ a. Mechanical, electrical, tidal, radiant, chemical
   - _____ b. Geothermal, electrical, nuclear, hydraulic, mechanical
   - _____ c. Radiant, chemical, electrical, thermal, mechanical
   - _____ d. Mechanical, electrical, thermal, cosmic, radioactive

2. The emergency flashers on a car work when the ignition is ON or OFF. The radio works only when the ignition is ON. Stepping on the brakes when the flashers are on provides power to the radio even when the switch is OFF. This is a:
   - _____ a. Sneak path
   - _____ b. Sneak condition
   - _____ c. Sneak label
   - _____ d. Sneak timing

3. A proper fault hazard analysis should consider:
   - _____ a. All faults
   - _____ b. All faults and their effects
   - _____ c. Only faults that have caused mishaps
   - _____ d. Faults which may have safety related effects

4. A fault hazard analysis should determine not only what can fail but also the manner in which it can fail.
   - _____ a. True
   - _____ b. False

5. One strategy to prevent an energy related mishap is to:
   - _____ a. Provide for the release of energy
   - _____ b. Separate the energy from other assets
   - _____ c. Accumulate the energy
   - _____ d. Eliminate energy blocks

6. Worksheets describing system behavior, including personnel actions, are a part of:
   - _____ a. Energy trace analysis
   - _____ b. Management oversight risk tree
   - _____ c. STEP analysis
   - _____ d. Energy concept analysis

7. The change analysis in MORT is used to compare an accident situation with an accident-free situation.
   - _____ a. True
   - _____ b. False

8. Management system less than adequate may be discovered by:
   - _____ a. Energy trace analysis
   - _____ b. Management oversight risk tree
   - _____ c. Step analysis
   - _____ d. Fault hazard analysis

9. A failure, mode and effect analysis is similar to:
   - _____ a. Energy trace analysis
   - _____ b. Management oversight risk tree
   - _____ c. Step analysis
   - _____ d. Fault hazard analysis

10. Tracking from the starting point through branches to use or transfer points is a part of:
    - _____ a. Energy trace analysis
    - _____ b. Management oversight risk tree
    - _____ c. Step analysis
    - _____ d. Energy concept analysis

11. Schematics may be used for sneak circuit analysis.
    - _____ a. True
    - _____ b. False

12. The input/output tracking of potentially harmful energy flows is a part of:
    - _____ a. Energy trace analysis
    - _____ b. Management oversight risk tree
    - _____ c. Step analysis
    - _____ d. Energy concept analysis

13. A fault hazard analysis considers:
    - _____ a. Function modes of failure
    - _____ b. Out-of-tolerance failure modes
    - _____ c. The effects of failures
    - _____ d. All of the above

14. It is sufficient to find one failure mode for each component being analyzed.
    - _____ a. True
    - _____ b. False

15. The concept that all losses are due to an interference in the normal transfer of energy is a part of:
    - _____ a. Energy trace analysis
    - _____ b. Management oversight risk tree
    - _____ c. Energy concept analysis
    - _____ d. Step analysis

8

Hazard Analysis II
Fault Tree Construction

Introduction

The concept of *fault tree analysis* is based on techniques originated by Bell Laboratories to describe the flow of "correct" logic in data processing. This technique was expanded by the Boeing Company while performing safety evaluations of the Minuteman missile, as a method for analyzing "false" logic which resulted from component failures and/or wrong commands. In addition, such a process has been shown to be ideally suited to the application of probability theory in the numerical evaluation of critical fault paths and modes. Many variations of the fault tree have appeared since 1960. Those presented here are only those required for a basic understanding of the principles now in general use.

Logic Symbols

Before proceeding in our discussion of the use of the fault tree diagram, we must first define the appropriate logic symbols. The fault tree is constructed from the "top down." The top of each logic symbol represents the output while the bottom represents the inputs.

Gates

The fault event that occurs as a result of malfunctions is contained in a box or rectangle, as shown in figure 8.1. This symbol is shown as the output of a gate.

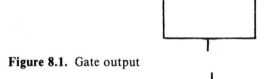

Figure 8.1. Gate output

Figure 8.2. AND gate

The AND gate, figure 8.2, describes the logical operation where the coexistence of all the inputs is required to produce the indicated output.

Figure 8.3. OR gate

The OR gate, figure 8.3, defines the condition where the output event will exist if at least one of the input events occur. That is to say, the output occurs if any one or more of the inputs occur.

There are no limitations to the number of inputs to either the AND or the OR gate, but each gate may have but one logical output.

A hexagon, figure 8.4, is used to symbolize the *inhibit* gate where a conditional relationship exists between one fault and another.

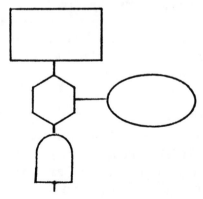

Figure 8.4. Inhibit gate

At the inhibit gate, the input event or fault produces the output event only if the indicated condition is satisfied. The conditional modifier to the inhibit gate is shown as an ellipse, as in figure 8.4, and the inhibit gate must always have a conditional modifier.

Faults

The circle describes basic fault inputs that require no further development. This category, depicted in figure 8.5, includes component failures whose frequency and failure mode are derived through testing.

Figure 8.5. Primary fault

The diamond, figure 8.6, describes fault inputs that may be considered basic only in a given fault tree. This event is not basic in the sense that failure data is available, but rather in the sense that the fault tree is developed no further, either because the substantiating evidence is unavailable, or because it appears that the event is of insufficient consequence to merit further refinement at the time of the fault tree preparation.

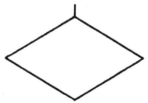

Figure 8.6. Secondary fault

Occasionally an undesired event will occur only in concert with some event that is not a fault. For example, the undesired event, "bartender runs out of beer at TGIF party," in addition to the fault events, requires the non-fault event "it is Friday." This type of event is shown as a "house" in figure 8.7.

Figure 8.7. Non-fault event

The triangle, with coding alpha-numerics, is used to indicate a continuation of a tree branch at another point. The same code is used at the temporary termination as at the restart of the branch, as shown in figure 8.8.

Figure 8.8. Transfer symbols

Personnel Involvement

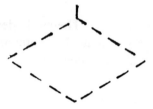

Figure 8.9. Personnel involvement

An additional refinement that is frequently used in fault trees is the use of dashed lines instead of solid lines to indicate an involvement of personnel. This will generally occur only on circles (primary faults) or diamonds (secondary faults).

Fault Tree Preparation

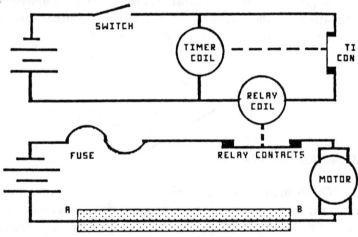

Figure 8.10. Wiring diagram

The actual preparation of a fault tree begins with the definition of the final "undesired" event, sometimes called the *head event*, and proceeds with a series of *a posteriori* judgments until basic input events are described.

As an example of the development of a fault tree, consider the wiring diagram shown in figure 8.10. A prior analysis has indicated that the overheating of the wire between points A and B is a critical event, due to the proximity of this section of the wire to ordnance. A fault tree is constructed to define the various failure modes by which this section of wire might become overheated.

Before attempting any analysis, it is necessary to learn how the system functions. This circuit is designed to make mechanical energy available from the motor when the switch is closed. When the switch is closed, power is applied to the relay coil through the timer contacts. The relay coil closes the relay contacts, which permits the current to flow through the fuse to the motor. When the switch is opened, the lack of power to the timer coil opens the timer contacts, removing power from the relay coil. This, in turn, opens the relay contacts and disrupts the flow of current to the motor.

If, for any reason, the switch should fail to open after some preset time interval, the timer contacts should open and remove power from the relay coil. If the motor fails shorted while the relay contacts are closed, the fuse should open and deenergize the circuit.

The *head* or undesired event is the overheating of the wire. Commencing with this event, the various causes are developed through paths that in combination produce the undesired event. In general, each cause should have a noun, a verb and a verbal modifier. The noun describes the mechanism, e.g., *the switch*; the verb states what happens, e.g, *fails*; and the modifier states the failure mode, e.g., *shorted* or *open*.

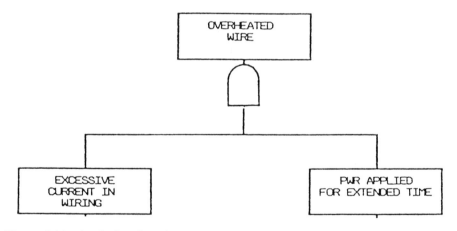

Figure 8.11. Analysis - Step 1

Overheating of the wire between A and B can occur only from the application of current beyond the rated capacity of the wire for an extended time. The co-existence of both an excessive current and an "over-run" condition are essential to produce the undesired head event. Using an AND gate, this is represented as shown in figure 8.11.

The event "excessive current in the system wiring" can occur if the motor fails shorted and if the fuse is unable to open. To combine these two events, an AND gate is used, as shown in figure 8.12. If the motor fails shorted and the fuse opens, there will, of course, be no excessive current. And if the motor does not fail shorted, there will also be no excessive current that can produce the overheating.

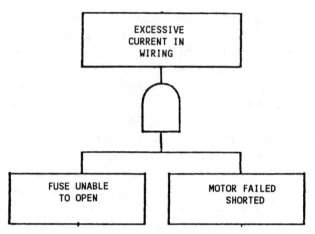

Figure 8.12. Analysis - Step 2

The other event that heads a path leading directly to the undesired event is "power applied to the system for an extended time." This event will occur only if the power is not removed from the relay coil, or if the relay fails in the closed condition, or if both events happen. This requires an OR gate, as shown in figure 8.13.

Each of the inputs to the gates shown in figures 8.11 and 8.12 are then developed further as to the events that lead to these occurrences. For simplification of the discussion, the paths will be considered separately, beginning with the "excessive current" event.

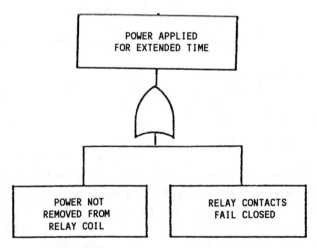

Figure 8.13. Analysis - Step 3

The AND events that can produce excessive current in the wiring are "fuse unable to open" and "motor failed shorted."

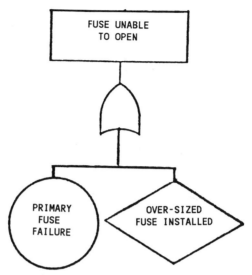

Figure 8.14. Analysis - Step 4

The first of these events can happen if there is a primary fuse failure, or it can happen if an oversized fuse had been installed. The two events that contribute to the fuse not opening consist of a primary fault (fuse failure) and a secondary fault (oversized fuse installed), figure 8.14.

This portion of the fault tree has now reached a decision point where the analyst must choose between two types of analysis. The analyst may decide to consider only the primary component failures, or he can break down the secondary failures to sub-causes. Primary failures are those that occur while the part or component is operating within the parameters for which it was designed, while secondary failures are those for which the component is subjected to abnormal, out-of-design stresses, such as being overheated from another component.

If the analyst is using the primary technique, the probability of the oversized fuse being installed will be added, if available, and no further action will be taken on the secondary failure. It may well be that the path through "fuse unable to open" is deemed critical, and if so, the analyst may decide to make a further breakdown of the secondary fault, "oversized fuse installed," to determine how, why and how often this could occur.

The other path leading down from "excessive current" is "motor failed shorted." The motor failure in this mode is a primary failure, so this branch of the tree is terminated at this point, as shown in figure 8.15, with a circle to indicate a primary failure.

In a similar manner, the other branch of the fault tree is developed for the events leading to both "power not removed from relay coil" and "relay contacts fail in the closed position." The latter event is due to a primary relay contact failure, and needs no further development, while the first event has additional elements to consider.

The portion of the fault tree leading to "relay contacts fail shorted" is shown in figure 8.16.

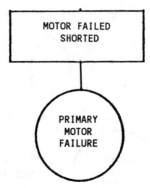

Figure 8.15. Analysis - Step 5

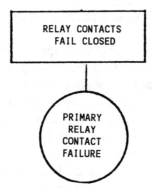

Figure 8.16. Analysis - Step 6

The event "power not removed from the relay coil" can occur if the timer is unable to open and the switch fails to open. The timer failure is due to a primary failure of the timer coil or a primary failure of the timer contacts.

The switch failing to open can be due to the switch contacts failing in the closed condition or the external control failing to release the switch.

The portion of the fault tree leading to "power not removed from the relay coil" is shown in figure 8.17.

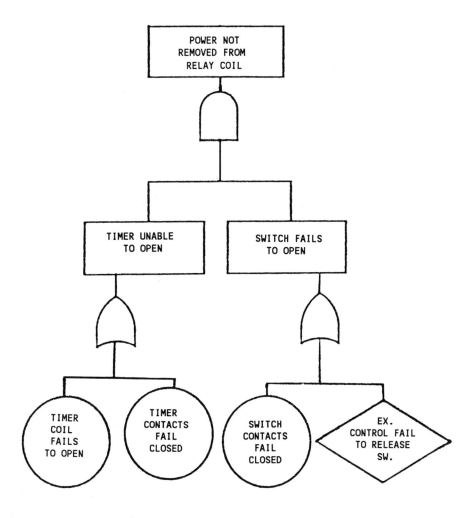

Figure 8.17. Analysis - Step 7

All of the portions that have been developed can be combined into a complete fault tree as shown in figure 8.18.

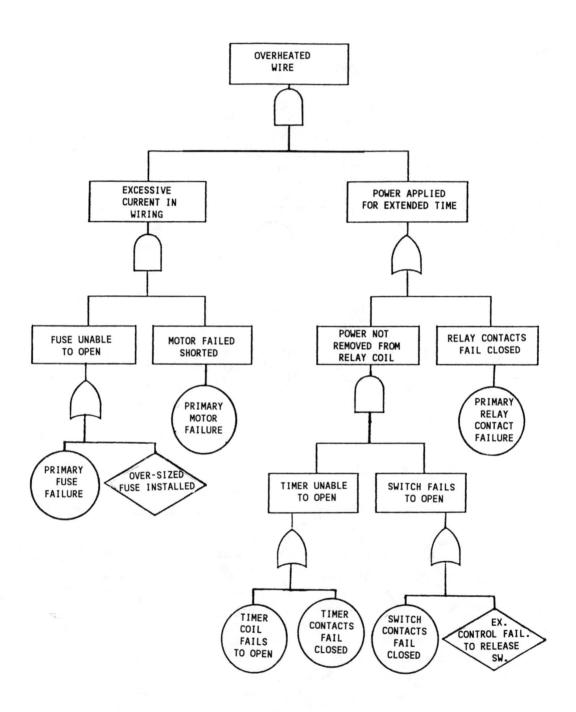

Figure 8.18. Wiring Fault Tree

Refinements

The preceding development has been made in the most simplistic manner possible as a demonstrative aid. An actual construction of a fault tree must consider in much greater depth the various facets of the development of the events.

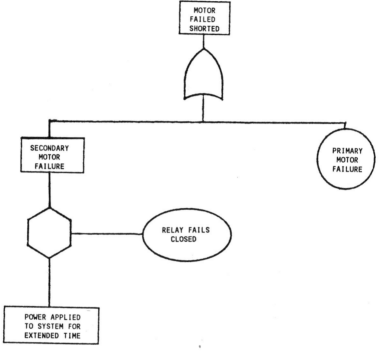

Figure 8.19. Use of Inhibit Gate

For example, in the AND gate leading to the event "excessive current in the system," the fuse must fail before the motor fails. In a similar manner, for the AND gate leading to "power not removed from the relay coil," the timer failure must precede the switch failure. In both of these cases, an inhibit gate with the appropriate modifier condition should be used.

If either of the above two events occur in reverse order, the system will fail in a mode unrelated to this fault tree. This emphasizes the point that the fault tree is constructed as a means of examining the critical faults leading to the selected undesired event. Some of the same faults and perhaps even some of the same fault paths may lead to some other undesired event, but that possibility is not being considered in this fault tree.

One thing that this simplistic approach can do is to point out critical paths and give some indication of the overall criticality of this fault tree. Note that an AND gate requires two or more events to happen in concert, and in general, paths through AND gates are less critical than paths through OR gates. For example, the secondary fault "oversized fuse installed" leads through an OR gate (some degree of criticality) to an AND gate (less critical). Even if an oversize fuse is installed, the event "excessive current in system wiring" can occur *only* if there is a primary motor failure. If there is a very low probability of this occurring, one need pay little attention to the probability of installing an oversize fuse.

With the primary failure technique, the failure of one component is presumed to be unrelated to the failure of any other component not in the same fault path. With the secondary failure technique, however, all significant inter-relationships must be developed. Of the five components with primary failures in figure 8.19, (motor, relay, timer, fuse and switch), it is possible that three are adequately defined as primary failures. In general, the fuse, timer and switch will be unaffected by a failure of any of the other components. The motor and the relay are, however, sensitive to the failure of one another. For example, "motor fails shorted" is likely to occur if the relay contacts remain closed and the motor continues to run for an extended time. In addition, if the motor fails shorted, the relay contacts may fail in the closed mode due to the excessive current.

To describe these secondary failures, it is convenient to use an inhibit gate to show the causal relationship between one fault and another. For the secondary failure technique with "motor failed shorted," there may be an input of both the primary motor failure, as before, or a secondary motor failure due to power being applied for an extended time with the relay contacts closed. The causal modifier to the inhibit gate is identical to the "right hand side" input to the undesired event. If this path is to be completed down the line, it would duplicate the right side of figure 8.19. There is nothing wrong in duplicating paths, but to avoid excessive diagramming, the triangle symbol, as shown in figure 8.8, is used to transfer to another part of the diagram. This symbol can be used not only for duplicate paths, but to transfer any portion of a path to an additional sheet of the diagram.

Self-Repair

As has been stated, only the elementary basics of fault tree construction have been presented. One technique that is used, but will not be discussed here in depth, is that of the self-repair. This is the case when the system "cures itself," such as bringing on a backup generator when the primary system fails. There are special methods to analyze self-repair situations, one of which is called the *lambda tau* method.

Introduction - Qualitative and Quantitative Analysis

A fault tree is a representation of failure events in a symbolic logic format, and analysis may be made in either qualitative (without numbers) or quantitative (numerical) methods. Even when a quantitative analysis is

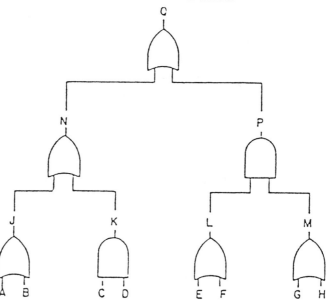

Figure 8.20. Generic Fault Tree

desired, a qualititative analysis is usually performed first. In fact, one might say that the very construction of a fault tree is a qualitative analysis.

Qualitative Analysis

For the generic fault tree shown in figure 8.20, starting at the head event, Q, note that Q will occur if either event N or event P (or both) occur. At this first level, note that a single event, N or P, will produce the undesired head event.

Continuing down the left branch of the fault tree, note that event N will occur if either J or K occur. Inasmuch as Q occurs if N occurs, then Q will occur if either J or N (or both) occur.

J is the outcome of an OR gate with input events (faults) A and B, and so J will occur if either A or B (or both) occur. Inasmuch as the occurrence of J produces the occurrence of Q, note that the undesired head event will occur if A occurs or if B occurs.

The other input to event N is K, which is the output of an AND gate involving C and D. That is to say, K will occur only if C and D occur. Thus two events must occur in this branch in order for N to occur, while in the other branch, either of two single faults could produce the outcome N.

Going down the right hand branch, the event P, being the output of an AND gate, occurs only when both L and M occur. L, in turn, will occur if either E or F (or both) occur, while M will occur with the occurrence of either G or H. Two events must occur before P occurs. These events are E and G, E and H, F and G or F and H.

Cut Sets

A *cut set* is a set, or path, of events that will lead from the basic, bottom line faults to the undesired Head Event. A *minimum cut set* is the shortest or most direct route between the basic faults and the head event.

In the previous illustration, we saw that the events that will produce the event Q are:

A; B; C and D; E and H; F and G; or F and H.

The path A-J-N-Q and the path B-J-N-Q are minimum cuts sets for this fault tree. This immediately gives the analyst a clue as to where to focus attention. If all other factors are equal, reducing the probability of occurrence of A and B should drastically change the probability of occurrence of the head event.

Single Point Failures

In the example, the failure of a single item (either A or B) produces the undesired event. Events A and B are, therefore, referred to as *single point failures*. Single point failures are always minimum cut sets, but minimum cut sets are not necessarily single point failures.

Quantitative Analysis

Boolean algebra may be used to express the outputs of events of a fault tree in terms of basic inputs, where the Boolean symbol $\cup$ stands for an OR event (called a *union*) and the symbol $\cap$ represents the AND event (called an *intersection*).

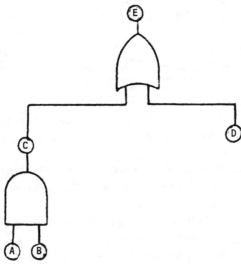

Figure 8.21. Quantitative Example

The logic tree of figure 8.21 can be expressed by the following Boolean algebra equations:

$$E = (C \cup D) \tag{1}$$
$$C = (A \cap B) \tag{2}$$

or

$$E = (A \cap B) \cup D \tag{3}$$

"E equals C *or* D" or "E equals C *union* D".

and   "C equals A *and* B" or "C equals A *intersection* B".

AND Events

The probability of the occurrence of an AND event (intersection) is the product of the probabilities of the causal events. This may be illustrated by a *probability tree.*

Let us assume that event A has two equal outcomes, one a success (S) and one a failure (F). Therefore, the probability of failure is one-half. (We shall consider only failures, since we are developing *fault* diagrams.) Let us suppose that there are three equal outcomes from B -- one a success and two failures. The probability of failure for event B is therefore two-thirds. For each outcome of A there are three possible outcomes of B, and these are shown on the probability tree in figure 8.22.

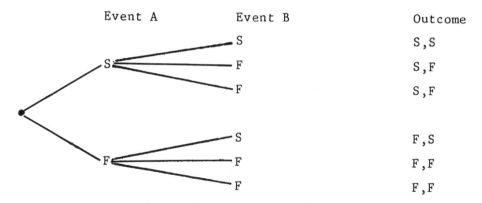

Figure 8.22. Probability Tree

From figure 8.22 we see there are six possible outcomes, of which two are both failures. The probability of A AND B (A intersection B) is therefore 2/6 or 1/3.

The same result could have been obtained by multiplying the probability of A by the probability of B.

$$P(AND \ B) = P(A \cup B) = P(A) \bullet P(B) = 1/2 \times 2/3 = 1/3 \tag{4}$$

and for the illustrative case,

P(A AND B) = 1/2 x 2/3 = 1/3
P(A AND B) = 1/2 x 2/3 = 1/3

Because of the multiplication of input probabilities through an AND gate, the symbol for this gate is sometimes shown with a multiplication "dot" (•) in the center.

OR Events

The probability of OR events is cumulative. That is to say, if the outcome depends on the failure of either one event or another (or both), the probability of the outcome is the sum of the probabilities of the input events.

If there is an overlap (intersection) of the two events being considered in OR events, this overlap must be considered so as not to count this portion of the events twice. For example, if one were to consider the probability of apples OR round fruit, one must not count the round fruit that are apples twice. As a result of this, the basic equation for an OR event is

$$P(A \cup B) = P(A \text{ OR } B) = P(A) + P(B) - P(A \cap B) \qquad (5)$$

For those events that are mutually independent, i.e., no overlap, the intersection term of equation (5) is equal to zero. For fault tree analysis, the intersection term of an OR equation is generally considered to be zero, whether or not the events are mutually independent. This is due to the fact that in most fault events, the probability of the fault is so low that the product term is insignificant when compared to the sum (OR) term.

Unlike the qualitative analysis, quantitative analysis commences with the lowest level and works upward.

$$P(J) = P(A) + P(B) = 0.001 + 0.002 \qquad = 0.003$$
$$P(K) = P(C) \bullet P(D) = 0.003 \ 0.004 \qquad = 0.000012$$
$$P(L) = P(E) + P(F) = 0.005 + 0.005 \qquad = 0.010$$
$$P(M) = P(G) + P(H) = 0.003 + 0.002 \qquad = 0.005$$

Working up the left branch,

$$P(N) = P(J) + P(K) = 0.003 + 0.000012 \qquad = 0.003012$$

and, on the right branch,

$$P(P) = P(L) \bullet P(M) = 0.010 \ 0.005 \qquad = 0.000050$$

so that the head event,

$$P(Q) = P(N) + P(P) = 0.003012 + 0.000050 \qquad = 0.003062$$

If all AND gate events had been dependent events, the head event probability would have been

$$P(Q) = 0.003060 \text{ vice } 0.003062$$

Not much change!

Quantitative Analysis of Example

With the minimum cut sets being A and B, an approximation to the entire fault tree can be made by a simplified tree containing only these two branches, as shown in figure 8.23.

Figure 8.23. Equivalent Fault Tree

Use of this simplified fault tree would give the probability of the head event as

$$P(Q) = P(A) + P(B) = 0.001 + 0.002 = 0.003$$

This answer varies from the "exact" answer by 2 percent.

Another way to demonstrate the minimum cut sets is by writing a single modified Boolean equation for the entire fault tree. Without the intermediate steps, showing only the event symbol and not the probability designator, this would be

$$Q = A + B + CD + EG + FG$$

and, again, by dropping the "higher order" terms, the probability of the head event is seen to be approximated by the sum of the probabilities of events A and B.

"High" AND Gates

The effect of an AND gate is to reduce the probability of failure. In this sense, an AND gate for a failure is analogous to a parallel circuit wherein both components must fail for overall failure of the subsystem.

Since the presence of an AND gate reduces the overall probability of failure, it stands to reason that the higher in the fault tree one finds an AND gate, the lower the probability of the head event. Thus, as a rule of thumb, AND gates near or at the top of fault tree diagrams are preferable, *except* consider the system shown in figure 8.24 for the inadvertent firing of the cartridge when the jettison switch is activated.

Here we see an AND gate at the very top of the fault tree, indicating that for the undesired head event to occur, there must be at least two failures, i.e., no single point failures.

However, note that one possible cut set, in the right hand branch is, from the top down:

1. K051 relay contact are closed
2. Relay K0 312 is energized
3. *28 Vdc present at pin c, P18.*

On the left hand branch, one possible cut set is:

1. 28 Vdc present at K051 contacts
2. *28 Vdc present at pin c, P18.*

A single point failure is disguised by its appearance in two places in the fault tree. And, even though there is an AND gate at the very top of the

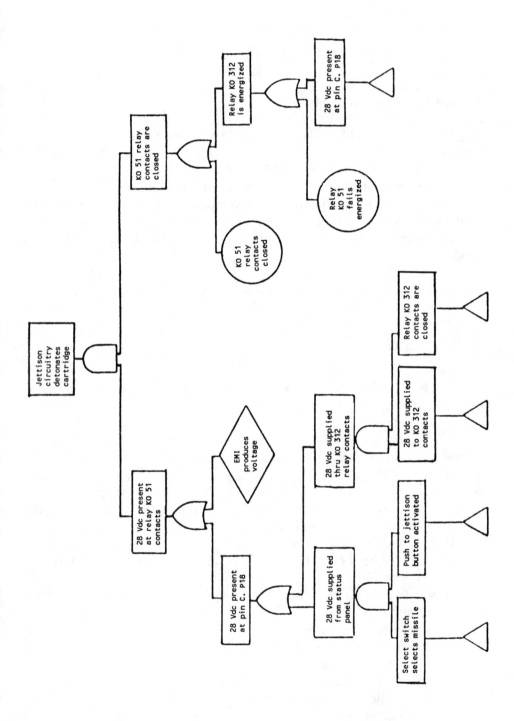

Figure 8.24. High AND Gate Fault Tree

diagram, the presence of this voltage at pin c, plug 18 causes the undesired event! It does not take much imagination to see the possibilities of this occurring in large multi-page fault trees unless some schema is devised to call out duplicate events.

Fault Tree Bibliography

Hammer, W. *Occupational Safety Management and Engineering*. Englewood Cliffs, NJ: Prentice-Hall, 1981.

U.S. Nuclear Regulatory Commission, 1981. *Fault Tree Handbook*. NUREG-0492. Washington: Office of Nuclear Safety and Safeguards, January.

Rowland, H. E., and B. Moriarity. *System Safety and Management*. New York: John Wiley and Sons, 1983.

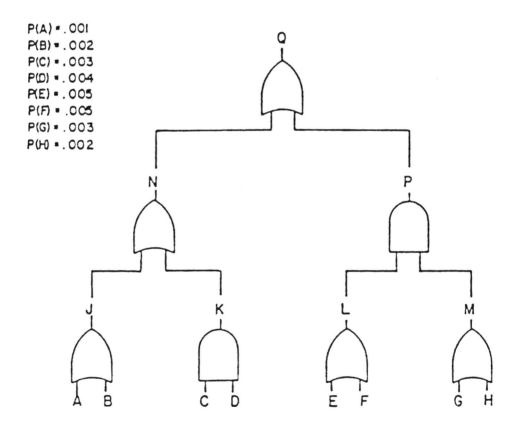

P(A) = .001
P(B) = .002
P(C) = .003
P(D) = .004
P(E) = .005
P(F) = .005
P(G) = .003
P(H) = .002

Figure 8.25. Generic Tree With Probabilities

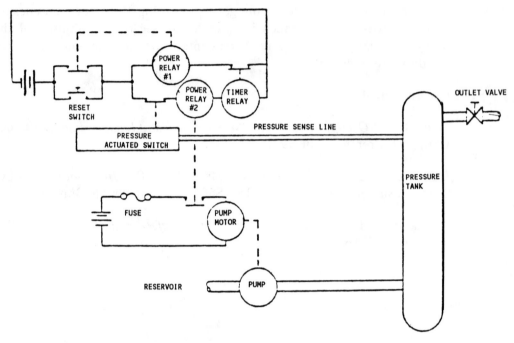

Figure 8.26. Pressure Tank Diagram

Additional Faults

1. Primary failure, reset switch
2. Pressure sense line leak
3. Relay contacts #1 fail
4. Pressure switch failure
5. Incorrect timer setting
6. Reset switch remains closed
7. Primary failure, timer relay
8. Primary failure, relay #1
9. Timer relay fails to open with pressure switch closed
10. Secondary failure, timer relay
11. External controls on reset fail

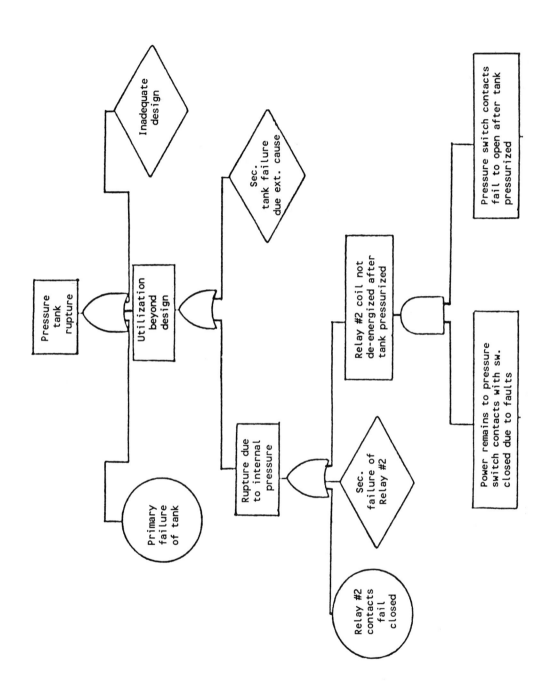

Figure 8.27. Partial Pressure Tank Tree

91

Self-Study Questions

1. The inhibit gate is used to describe:
   - _____ a. Critical paths
   - _____ b. Conditional faults
   - _____ c. Self-repair modes
   - _____ d. Secondary failures

2. The "house" symbol in a fault tree denotes:
   - _____ a. A preliminary fault
   - _____ b. A conditional fault
   - _____ c. A non-fault
   - _____ d. A secondary fault

3. A fault tree is conducted from the *top* down.
   - _____ a. True
   - _____ b. False

4. The "no further development" of the diamond symbol is used if:
   - _____ a. No information is available as to that fault
   - _____ b. Events leading up to that fault are not known
   - _____ c. It is anticipated that this event may not be critical
   - _____ d. All of the above

5. A single point failure:
   - _____ a. Can not be below an OR gate
   - _____ b. Can not be below an AND gate
   - _____ c. Can not occur in more than one branch of a tree
   - _____ d. Is not a minimum cut set

6. For the system shown in figure 8.26 and the partial fault tree shown in figure 8.27, the causes of the event "Pressure switch contacts fail to open after tank pressurized," does not include:
   - _____ a. Primary failure, timer relay
   - _____ b. Pressure sense line leak
   - _____ c. Pressure switch primary failure
   - _____ d. Pressure switch secondary failure

7. For the above system, the gate below the event "Pressure switch contacts fail to open after tank pressurized" is:
   - _____ a. OR gate
   - _____ b. AND gate
   - _____ c. Conditional gate
   - _____ d. Primary gate

8. The failure in the closed condition of the contact of Relay 2 of Problem F is a single point failure.
   _____ a. True
   _____ b. False

9. Other than secondary failures, what are the minimum cut set(s) of Problem F?
   _____ a. Primary failure of the tank only
   _____ b. Relay #2 contacts fail closed
   _____ c. Both answers 1 and 2
   _____ d. Neither answer 1 nor 2

10. How can you be certain that the "unfinished" portion of figure 8.27 does not contain minimum cut set(s)?
    _____ a. The additional faults feed into an OR gate
    _____ b. All the additional faults are not Primary faults
    _____ c. There may not be OR gates in the additional faults
    _____ d. The additional faults feed into an AND gate

11. If the probability of a primary failure of the tank is 0.00003, what is the approximate probability of the pressure tank rupture?
    _____ a. .00017
    _____ b. .00023
    _____ c. .000000008
    _____ d. .000032

12. For the system shown in figure 8.18, there are no single point failures.
    _____ a. True
    _____ b. False

13. Which is a minimum cut set of the system of problem L?
    _____ a. Fuse failure, motor failure, over-sized fuse
    _____ b. Fuse failure, motor failure, relay contact failure
    _____ c. Fuse failure, over-sized fuse, relay contact failure
    _____ d. Over-sized fuse, timer coil, relay contacts

14. For the system represented in figure 8.21, the cuts sets are:
    _____ a. A, B, D
    _____ b. AB, D
    _____ c. B, A, D
    _____ d. ABD

15. For the above system, P(A) = 0.002; P(B) = .004; P(D) = .006.
    _____ a. P(E) = .012
    _____ b. P(E) = .006
    _____ c. P(E) = .006008
    _____ d. P(E) = .0036

9

Risk Management

Introduction

Even if the hazards can be identified, it is usually impossible to eliminate, or even control, all of the hazards of a system. This may be due to restraints on funding and other resources, the difficulty in eliminating the hazards, or the relative insignificance of the hazards. It is therefore necessary to make some value judgment as to what hazards should be considered for primary elimination or control emphasis. Thus it is that the system safety practitioner must be able to present to management some type of rationale for the management of the risks associated with the detected hazards.

In the early stages of a system life cycle, the severity of a hazard is generally the only clue as to how important the hazard may be. This is because even though hazards may be detected at this point, the probability of the occurrence of the hazards may not have been determined as yet. Even the severity of the hazards may be known only in gross terms, and therefore a rating such as used in MIL STD 882B will be sufficient for this first cut at risk assessment. This severity listing is repeated in Table 9.1.

Table 9.1
MIL STD 882B Hazard Severity

Category	Description	Mishap Definition
I	Catastrophic	Death or system loss
II	Critical	Severe injury, severe occupational illness or major system damage
III	Marginal	Minor injury, minor occupational illness, or minor system damage
IV	Negligible	Less than minor injury, occupational illness or system damage

As the design of the system progresses, one should be able to determine the expected frequency of occurrence of the hazard with some degree of accuracy, or at least with some degree of repeatability. This frequency may be either relativistic or probabilistic.

Once again, in the early phases of a program, relativistic information may be all that is available, and even in later phases, probabilistic data may not be always available for all components and all sub-systems.

An example of relativistic hazard probability is also given in MIL STD 882B, and is repeated in Table 9.2.

Table 9.2
MIL STD 882B Hazard Probability

Level	Description	Fleet/Inventory*
A	Frequent	Likely to occur frequently
B	Probable	Will occur several times in the life of an item
C	Occasional	Likely to occur sometime in the life of an item
D	Remote	Unlikely, but possible to occur in life of an item
E	Improbable	So unlikely, it can be assumed occurrence may not be experienced.

* The size of the inventory should be defined.

Risk Assessment Matrices

Overview Matrix

With a determination of both hazard severity and hazard probability, it is possible to draw up a risk assessment matrix to aid in the decision of which risks require the most attention. Such a matrix may also be used to determine at what management level the risk acceptance decision must be made.

A broad overview risk matrix is shown in figure 9.1. The general descriptive terms used in the matrix do little to cue the analyst as to where to place the hazard reduction emphasis. Observe that the top three frequencies under catastrophic severity, the top two frequencies under critical severity, and the most frequent occurrence for a marginal category all have the same design action listed.

HAZARD SEVERITY		A FREQUENT	B PROBABLE	C OCCASIONAL	D REMOTE	E IMPROBABLE	F IMPOSSIBLE
I CATASTROPHIC		A-4 DESIGN ACTION REQUIRED TO ELIMINATE OR CONTROL HAZARD	B-4 DESIGN ACTION REQUIRED TO ELIMINATE OR CONTROL HAZARD	C-4 DESIGN ACTION REQUIRED TO ELIMINATE OR CONTROL HAZARD	D-4 HAZARD MUST BE CONTROLLED OR HAZARD PROBA-BILITY REDUCED		
II CRITICAL		A-3 DESIGN ACTION REQUIRED TO ELIMINATE OR CONTROL HAZARD	B-3 DESIGN ACTION REQUIRED TO ELIMINATE OR CONTROL HAZARD	C-3 HAZARD MUST BE CONTROLLED OR HAZARD PROBA-BILITY REDUCED	D-3 HAZARD CONTROL DESIRABLE IF COST EFFECTIVE	ASSUME WILL NOT OCCUR	IMPOSSIBLE OCCURENCE
III MARGINAL		A-2 DESIGN ACTION REQUIRED TO ELIMINATE OR CONTROL HAZARD	B-2 HAZARD MUST BE CONTROLLED OR HAZARD PROBA-ABILITY REDUCED	C-2 HAZARD CONTROL DESIRABLE IF	D-2 NORMALLY NOT COST EFFECTIVE		
IV NEGLIGIBLE				NEGLIGIBLE HAZARD			

HAZARD PROBABILITY

Figure 9.1. Hazard criticality matrix

Weighted Matricies

Perhaps a better approach would be that shown in the risk assessment matrix shown in figure 9.2. Here one sees that a risk assessment code (RAC) has been assigned based on a severity-probability weighting. From figure 9.2 one would deduce that, all other things being equal, primary emphasis should be placed on the RAC 1 items, i.e., "Catastrophic and critical -- likely to occur immediately" and "Catastrophic -- probably will occur in time."

A slightly expanded version of this matrix is shown as figure 1 of MIL STD 882B, Appendix A. In this matrix, of the twenty (20) possible relationships, [five (5) frequency ratings times four (4) severity ratings], six (6) are listed as unacceptable and five (5) are listed as undesirable.

MISHAP PROBABILITY

HAZARD SEVERITY		A LIKELY TO OCCUR IMMEDIATELY	B PROBABLY WILL OCCUR IN TIME	C MAY OCCUR IN TIME	D UNLIKELY TO OCCUR
I CATASTROPHIC	MAY CAUSE DEATH OR SYSTEM LOSS	1 IMMINENT	1 RISK ASSESSMENT CODE	2	3
II CRITICAL	MAY CAUSE SEVERE INJURY OR DAMAGE	DANGER 1	2	3	4
III MARGINAL	MAY CAUSE MINOR INJURY OR DAMAGE	2	3	4	5
IV NEGLIGIBLE	PROBABLY WILL NOT AFFECT SAFETY	5	5	5	5

Figure 9.2. Risk assessment matrix

A second example of a risk assessment matrix is also presented in Appendix A of MIL STD 882B, and is shown here as figure 9.3. This matrix does not differ significantly from the other MIL STD 882B matrix, inasmuch as both matrices have twenty (20) imbedded points with five (5) listed as unacceptable, four (4) as undesirable and three (3) as acceptable. The only difference lies in the number of undesirable and acceptable with review points.

CATEGORY

FREQUENCY		CATASTROPHIC I	CRITICAL II	MARGINAL III	NEGLIGIBLE IV
	FREQUENT A	1	3	7	13
	PROBABLE B	2	5	9	15
	OCCASIONAL C	4	6	11	18
	REMOTE D	8	10	14	19
	IMPROBABLE E	12	16	17	20

1 - 5 UNACCEPTABLE   10 - 17 ACCEPTABLE WITH REVIEW
6 - 9 UNDESIRABLE   18 - 20 ACCEPTABLE, NO REVIEW

Figure 9.3. MIL STD 882B matrix

Use of the Risk Assessment Codes

There are several problems involved with the use of risk assessment matrices as previously shown. First of all, the consequences of the occurrences are given in gross terms with no direct provision for fine-tuning of the severity of the happenings. For example, the scope and depth of the severity term *critical* ranges from just slightly worst than *marginal* to almost *catastrophic*. It would be of great assistance if the severity indicators were subdivided. In a like manner, the frequency of occurrence is in overly broad terms and does not separate the probability of a hazardous occurrence from the exposure of the system to that hazard. For example, a system may have a high probability of failure under extreme heat conditions, but may have minimal failure possibility under conditions of cold.

In addition, one should include as either an implicit or explicit portion of the risk matrix some evaluation of the risk reduction process. This should include the cost of the risk reduction process and an evaluation of how much of the risk is being reduced.

An example of the use of a risk acceptance code as a management tool is shown in table 9.3 where guidelines are offered for a risk matrix similar to that shown in figure 9.2.

Table 9.3
Guidelines for risk matrix

RAC	ACTION
1	Elimination or positive control of the fault causing this hazard is imperative.
2	Elimination or positive control of the fault causing this hazard is highly desireable.
3	If the fault producing this hazard can not be eliminated, some control over the effect should be exercised.
4	Minimal effort should be expanded on correcting this fault.
5	No effort need be expended on correcting this fault.

Another application of the risk assessment code is taken by the U.S. Army, where the RAC is used to determine decision authority for the acceptance of unresolved hazards. This application is in table 9.4 for a risk matrix of MIL STD 882B severity (I, II, etc.) and frequency (A, B, etc.), for an aviation system being produced under the authority of the Army Systems Acquisition Review Council (ASARC), the Army Material Command (AMC), the Aviation Systems Command (AVSCOM), and the Program Manager (PM).

Table 9.4
Army use of Risk Assessment Code

Risk Code	Decision Authority
IA, IB, IC, IIA, IIB, IIC	Risk acceptance by ASARC
ID, IIC, IID, IIIB, IIIC	Risk acceptance by CDR AMC
IE, IIE, IIID, IIIE, IVA, IVB	Risk acceptance by CDR AVSCOM
IVC, IVD, IVE	Risk acceptance by PM

Criticality

The risk matrices and the risk assessment codes are tools to be used by management in making decisions as to where to make changes in a system. But even if an easy decision can be reached as to where to concentrate efforts, what type of change to make may well pose a greater problem than where to make the change.

One method for determining the utility of a change is through the development of a cost/benefit ratio. Unless one has very strong data to support the developed ratio, the ratio may be a somewhat vague entity, but it is usually possible to make a decision between two changes by comparing their criticality.

Negative Utility Factor

Negative utility factor, u_i, is the concept of a negative payoff (cost) for an occurrence, such as the cost in dollars or in personnel well-being associated with a mishap. This factor depends on the severity of the mishap, and even though it may be derived somewhat arbitrarily, if used in a consistent manner it can produce meaningful comparisons. The negative utility factor may be based on dollar cost, social cost or a relative index relationship. An example of the latter is shown in Table 9.5.

Table 9.5
Relative Index Relationship

Severity	Negative Utility Factor
First Aid	20
Temporary Total Disability	345
Permanent Partial Disability	2,500
Permanent Total Disability	21,000

Expected Negative Utility

Expected negative utility, E, is the summation of the product of probability of the occurrence of the ith severity class, P_i, and the negative utility factor for each class, u_i. If there are n classes, the expected negative utility for the event, if it occurs is

$$E = \sum_{i=1}^{} P_i u_i \qquad (1)$$

It is to be noted that equation (1) gives the expected negative utility of the event *if it occurs*. The value of E, therefore, is the "cost" of a mishap if it should occur. E may be expressed in dollars, number of damaged systems, lost work time, a relative index value, etc.

Criticality

In order to determine the total effect of the damage/loss, one must also consider the probability of the occurrence of the basic event. The *criticality,* C, of an event is the product of the probability of the occurrence of the event, P, and the expected negative utility, E:

$$C = P E \qquad (2)$$

Consider the criticality of the loss of the hydraulic system on an aircraft. From mishap reports or from hazard analyses, such as a fault tree analysis, it has been determined that the probability of the loss of the hydraulic system per 100,000 hours of flight is 2×10^{-8} ($P = 2 \times 10^{-8}$.).

A listing of the probability for each damage category (p_i) *if hydraulics are lost,* is shown in table 9.6.

Table 9.6
Probability of damage

Type of Damage	Probability of Occurrence
Minor	7.5×10^{-4}
Moderate	2.0×10^{-4}
Severe	4.0×10^{-5}
Loss of Aircraft	1.0×10^{-5}

Note that these probabilities do not add up to 1.0 because many of the occurrences due to loss of hydraulics do not result in a reportable mishap.

Another relationship has been developed with the negative utility factors that have been assigned for each mishap category. This is shown in table 9.7.

Table 9.7
Negative utility assigned to each mishap category

Damage	Negative Utility Factor
Minor	20
Moderate	100
Severe	1,000
Loss of Aircraft	20,000

The expected negative utility can now be computer for each damage category by multiplying the probability of occurrence by the corresponding negative utility factor. The expected negative utilities are shown in table 9.8.

Table 9.8
Expected negative utilities

P_i	u_i	E_i
7.5×10^{-4}	20	1.5×10^{-2}
2.0×10^{-4}	100	2.0×10^{-2}
4.0×10^{-5}	1,000	4.0×10^{-2}
1.0×10^{-5}	20,000	20.0×10^{-2}
		$E = 27.5 \times 10^{-2}$

Based on a probability of losing the hydraulics (P) equal to 2×10^{-8}, the criticality of the loss of hydraulics is:

$$C = P\,E = 2 \times 10^{-8}\ 27.5 \times 10^{-2} = 5.5 \times 10^{-9}$$

If the expected negative utility index were in thousands of dollars, one could expect a dollar loss of 5.5×10^{-6} per 100,000 hours of flight due to a loss of hydraulics. Except for an actuarial point of view, this figure may not have much meaning by itself, but it can become very meaningful when used in a comparison with other criticality figures.

However, even without considering other criticality numbers, some information can be gained from an examination of the expected negative utility values of table 9.8. It can be seen from these figures that the probability of having a severe accident, if the hydraulics fail, is much smaller than having a minor or moderate accident. Yet the "cost" of this category is at least four times as great. This, in itself, gives a strong indication as to what area might have a greater payoff if the accident probability could be reduced.

Now let us suppose that two alternative change proposals are under consideration for reducing the accident potential when hydraulics are lost. Estimates are prepared for the portability of each mishap category under each alternative, and criticality numbers are computed for each alternative. Alternative A has a criticality value of 5.4×10^{-9} and alternative B has a value of 4.2×10^{-9}. If all other factors (cost, effect on mission, etc.) were the same for both changes, one would tend to accept alternative B.

Self-Study Questions

1. Using the risk matrix of figure 9.2, what RAC would indicate an imperative necessity for positive control if the fault cannot be eliminated?
   - _____ a.   RAC 1
   - _____ b.   RAC 2
   - _____ c.   RAC 3
   - _____ d.   RAC 4

2. For this risk matrix, what RAC indicates minimal effort should be expended in fault alleviation?
   - _____ a.   RAC 1
   - _____ b.   RAC 2
   - _____ c.   RAC 3
   - _____ d.   RAC 4

3. For this risk matrix, if the RAC is 4, the fault should not be corrected.
   - _____ a.   True
   - _____ b.   False

4. A risk assessment code is assigned based on:
   - _____ a.   Hazard severity only
   - _____ b.   Hazard probability only
   - _____ c.   Weighted severity/probability relationship
   - _____ d.   Single point failures

5. A negative utility factor is:
   - _____ a.   A measure of the ease of mishap cost calculation
   - _____ b.   A designation of the type of mishap cost
   - _____ c.   The exact cost of a mishap
   - _____ d.   A "concept" for quantifying the "cost" of a mishap

6. The primary use of a risk assessment matrix is:
   - _____ a.   To determine the expected frequency of occurrence
   - _____ b.   As an aid in the decision process
   - _____ c.   To define severity and probability of an inventory
   - _____ d.   To develop failure events in a logical format

7. An example of a _relativistic_ hazard probably is:
   - _____ a.   Critical
   - _____ b.   Marginal
   - _____ c.   Frequent
   - _____ d.   Catastrophic

8. The criticality developed from the negative utility factor and the expected negative utility is:
   _____ a. A representation of the seriousness of a potential mishap
   _____ b. The dollar cost of a potential mishap
   _____ c. A quantification of hazard severity
   _____ d. A quantification of hazard probability

9. Risk management is a process that includes:
   _____ a. Determination of which risks to eliminate
   _____ b. Determination of which risks to control
   _____ c. Determination of the benefit of risk mitigation
   _____ d. All of the above

10. Early in a program, risk assessment is usually based on hazard severity alone.
    _____ a. True
    _____ b. False

11. The concept of a representation of a mishap cost in real dollars or in a relative index format is called:
    _____ a. Reverse cost analysis
    _____ b. Negative utility factor
    _____ c. Comparative utility analysis
    _____ d. Mishap consistency concept

12. A mishap that produces severe injury is assigned Category:
    _____ a. I
    _____ b. II
    _____ c. III
    _____ d. IV

13. The hazard severity categories of MIL STD 882 are sufficient for all analyses, and no modification needs to be made.
    _____ a. True
    _____ b. False

14. The cost of risk reduction process:
    _____ a. Should never enter into risk assessment
    _____ b. May be only an implicit consideration
    _____ c. May be an explicit consideration
    _____ d. Is a part of the risk assessment process

15. If quantitative hazard probabilities have been obtained:
    _____ a. A risk assessment matrix can not be used
    _____ b. A risk assessment matrix will provide precise RAC's
    _____ c. A modified risk assessment matrix should be constructed
    _____ d. The probabilities should be converted to qualitative

10

System Safety Control

Introduction

Control over a system safety program must commence early in the system life cycle. In fact, if there is an exploratory development cycle that precedes the development of the actual system, system safety should be considered during this research phase.

Program control takes many forms, ranging from formal contract documentation requirements to informal assessments. The following is an overview of some of the control actions.

Contractual Requirements

Tailored system safety requirements should be specified in contractual provisions, including the *statement of work* (SOW), bidder's instructions, *contract data requirements list* (CDRL), general and special contract provision sections, annexes, and other contractual means.

Tailoring of requirements refers to adjusting the scope and depth of safety activity, including reporting, to fit the needs of the program. Additional discussion of tailoring will be in a later part of this chapter

Statement of Work

The detailed requirements for the completion of a contracted project are contained in a *statement of work*. This document is used to amplify and/or detail the requirements of the MIL STD, along with the CDRL's.

Managing Activity Responsibilities

The managing activity is charged to establish, plan, organize and implement a system safety program that is integrated into all life cycle phases. This requires the establishment of definitive program requirements for the procurement or development of a system, including design requirements that are available and applicable, and acceptable risk levels.

Data

Safety data should be used as an aid to prevent design deficiencies, particularly those of a repetitive nature. Safety data are accumulated from prior programs, similar systems, earlier work on an on-going program, and other historical sources. The data are used to evaluate the safety of a system or verify compliance with the system safety requirements. These data include mishap reports, mishap probabilities, failure rates, test results, system safety analyses, failure mode and effect analyses, and human factors data. MIL STD 882B requires the documentation of these data and the retention of selected documented data.

As an example of the requirements for data, consider mishap reporting. Task 101 system safety program plan states, "The contractor shall describe in the SSPP the mishap ... analysis process including alerting the managing activity." Mishap reporting is also mentioned in demonstration and validation phase: "Evaluate results of safety tests, failure analyses and *mishap investigations* performed during the demonstration and validation phase." Similar statements are contained in the full-scale engineering phase and the production and deployment phase.

Deliverable Data

Data is termed *deliverable* if it is required to be furnished to the managing activity by the contractor. The instrument for requiring the data is the *contract data requirements list* (CDRL). If the CDRL does not specify deliverable data, it will not be delivered. Figure 10.1 is a sample of CDRL.

Non-Deliverable Data

Non-deliverable data is indexed, filed and maintained by the contractor for a specified time and is available at the contractor's facility for review and use by authorized representatives of the MA *upon request*, as specified in the CDRL.

Proprietory Data

In general, *proprietory data* refers to all data that is neither deliverable or non-deliverable. It used to be that all the data not specifically required by the managing activity was considered to be the exclusive property of the contractor. Recent court decisions, however, have ruled that anything developed by a company under contract to the U. S. Government belongs to the Government.

Data Item Descriptions

For those reports that have become "standardized," such as assessment reports and the system safety program plan, the description of the format is contained in a document called the *data item description* (DID). The information and format of a report may be tailored by amendments to the DID.

System Safety DID's

DI-SAFT-80100	System Safety Program Plan
DI-SAFT-80101	System Safety Hazard Analysis Report
DI-SAFT-80102	Safety Assessment Report
DI-SAFT-80103	Engineering Change Proposal System Safety Report
DI-SAFT-80104	Waiver or Deviation System Safety Report
DI-SAFT-80105	System Safety Program Progress Report
DI-SAFT-80106	Occupational Health Hazard Assessment Report

Program Control Tasks

Several of the tasks in the 2XX series (design and evaluation) require actions on the part of the contractor that will provide information to the managing activity to assist in the control of the program. These tasks are summarized below.

Task 206 - Occupational Health Hazard Assessment

This task requires the contractor to identify health hazards and to recommend engineering controls, equipment and/or protective procedures to reduce the associated risk to a level acceptable to the MA. Typical health hazards include toxic materials and physical agents that require system, facility and personnel protective equipment design requirements.

Task 207 - Safety Verification

Invoking this task requires the contractor to verify compliance with safety requirements on managing activity defined safety critical items. Compliance is

CONTRACT DATA REQUIREMENTS LIST

ATCH NR ________ TO EXHIBIT ________

TO CONTRACT PR ________________

CATEGORY ________________________

SYSTEM ITEM ________________________

CONTRACTOR ________________________

1. SEQUENCE NUMBER	2. TITLE OR DESCRIPTION OF DATA 3. SUBTITLE		6. TECHNICAL OFFICE			10. FREQUENCY	12. DATE OF 1ST SUBMISSION	14. DISTRIBUTION AND ADDRESSEES (Addressee – Regular Copies Repro Copies)	
4. AUTHORITY (*Data Item Number*)		5. CONTRACT REFERENCE	7. DD250 REQ	8. APP CODE (A)	9. INPUT TO IAC (X)	11. AS OF DATE	13. DATE OF SUBSEQUENT SUBM/EVENT ID		
1.	2. 3.		6.			10.	12.	14.	
4.		5.	7.	8.	9.	11.	13.		
16. REMARKS									15. TOTAL
1.	2. 3.		6.			10.	12.	14.	
4.		5.	7.	8.	9.	11.	13.		
16. REMARKS									15. TOTAL
1.	2. 3.		6.			10.	12.	14.	
4.		5.	7.	8.	9.	11.	13.		
16. REMARKS									15. TOTAL
1.	2. 3.		6.			10.	12.	14.	
4.		5.	7.	8.	9.	11.	13.		
16. REMARKS									15. TOTAL

PREPARED BY	DATE	APPROVED BY	DATE

DD FORM 1 JAN 75 1423 S/N 0102-LF-014-2300

REPLACES EDITION OF 1 JUN 68, WHICH IS USABLE.

PAGE ____ OF ____ PAGES

Figure 10.1. Data Item Descriptions

primarily in the form of safety testing, but engineering analyses, analogy, laboratory test, functional mockups or subscale/model simulation may be used when approved by the managing activity.

Task 208 - Training

Two facets of training are covered by this MIL STD Task, a training program for certification of test, operating and support personnel, and a training program for specific types and levels of contractor personnel, (managers, engineers and technicians), involved in design, product assurance, test and production. Contractor safety training shall also include government personnel who will be involved in contractor activities.

Task 209 - Safety Assessment

The contractor, under the requirements of this task, performs a safety assessment to identify all safety features and procedural hazards that may be present in the system. The safety assessment should summarize the safety criteria, methodology, analyses and tests used to identify hazards inherent in the system.

The contractor should identify those hazards that still have a residual risk and the actions taken to reduce the risk. He should give results of tests conducted to validate safety requirements; a list of all significant hazards (categorized as to whether or not they may be expected under normal or abnormal operating conditions); and specific safety recommendations or precautions required to ensure safety or personnel and property.

The safety assessment also reports any hazardous materials generated by or used in the system, and safety precautions and procedures necessary during system use, storage, transportation and disposal.

The safety assessment is concluded with a signed statement that all identified hazards have been eliminated, or their associated risks controlled to levels contractually specified as acceptable, and that the system is ready to test or operate or proceed to the next acquisition phase.

Task 210 - Safety Compliance Assessment

Task 210, when imposed, requires the contractor to perform and document a safety compliance assessment to identify and document compliance with appropriate design and operational safety requirements.

This assessment differs from that required in Task 209 in that this assessment concerns itself with the activities undertaken to follow contractual requirements rather than the evaluation of the safety results, as in Task 209.

Task 211 - Review of ECP's and Requests for Deviation/Waiver

Task 211 requires a safety analysis and evaluation of each *engineering change proposal* (ECP), as well as an analysis of each request for a deviation waiver to determine the hazards and assess the risk of the proposed deviation from or waiver of a requirement. When the level of safety of the system will be reduced by a deviation from or waiver of the requirement, method or process, the managing activity must be so notified.

Tailoring of a System Safety Program

The principal way to adjust the requirements of MIL STD 882B to provide a successful, cost-effective system safety program is by task selection and task adjustment. This process is called *tailoring*.

The general procedure, both for a contracted and an in-house program, is to start with an overall selection of the program management and control (Tasks 1XX) tasks and the design and evaluation (Tasks 2YY) tasks. By selecting certain tasks and "de-selecting" the remainder, one makes the initial "rough cut of the material." The selected tasks are then refined by careful specification of the "Details to be Specified by the MA" [Task XXX.3].

For example, let us consider that the contractual agreements have included the requirements to perform Task 103 - system safety program review. Section 103.3 of this task provides the platform for the managing activity to specify details as to how this task is to be conducted. These details for this task are:

(1) Set up a system safety program [Task 100]
(2) Set up a program review [Task 103]
    b. "identification of reviews, their content and probable location(s)"
    c. "...documenting..."
    d. "...schedule..."
    e. "...data delivery..."

Consider now that this task has been imposed in a program to build a trainer aircraft. The managing activity may desire:

- safety preliminary reviews
- critical design reviews
- a safety review of the preliminary evaluation
- a safety review of the technical evaluation
- a first flight readiness review for safety

All of these reviews have to be specified in the statement of work (SOW), along with a method for documenting the results of the review (perhaps different for each review), and the schedule for the reviews (some of which have to mesh with similar reviews for other disciplines). The data delivery schedule must be specified by the managing activity in the SOW and the CDRL. The review teams will probably be large and will vary from review to review.

Now let us suppose that this task has been exercised in a contract to build an airborne weapon launcher. The managing activity may desire only one, in-progress review plus a first-flight readiness (Approval for Service Use) review. The reviews may well consist of just one representative from the contractor and one from the managing activity. Documentation (while still an essential part of the program) will be much more simple, and perhaps only the "bottom line" need be documented. The difference between the use of Task 103 in these two extremes is accommodated in the statement of work and the contract data requirements list.

The selection of specific details in the task represents the "fine cuts" in the tailoring process.

Rationale for Task Selection

The managing activity chooses the tasks from MIL STD 882B to be imposed under the contractual agreements. One must keep in mind at all times that each task adds an extra cost to the program, and if a task is not *absolutely* essential it should *not* be included. If a task has only a partial need, then it should be evaluated to ascertain whether is should be (a) included, *in toto;* (b) not included at all; or (c) included but tailored so as to require only the elements of that task essential to the particular program.

The following is a capsulated summary of the rationale for each of the MIL STD Tasks:

Program Management and Control Tasks

TASK 100 - This task is required to initiate the entire program. It must be carefully tailored, especially for small programs.

TASK 101 - The contractor's "battle plan," this task not only tells the MA how the contractor is planning to run his safety program, but, by being prepared by the contractor safety personnel and being signed by the contractor management, the system safety program plan is the safety group's license to operate.

TASK 102 - This task is needed to bring together the safety activities of subs, associates and integrators. If there is but a prime contractor, this task is not required.

TASK 103 - This task has just been discussed under "Tailoring." A summary is contained in paragraph 50.1.4.3:" ... make sure all system safety open items are covered ...".

TASK 104 - This task provides for establishment of special safety groups and system safety working groups, including the naming of names or titles (if desired), and especially the naming of the chairman.

TASK 105 - Of utmost importance here is the procedure (established by the MA) for closing out hazard action items. This task makes use of the hazard log.

TASK 106 - This task establishes a test and evaluation program. It must be initiated early in the program!

TASK 107 - This task determines when, what and to whom progress reports should be issued.

TASK 108 - Are there minimum qualification requirements for system safety personnel? If so, the requirements should be set forth in this task.

Design and Engineering Tasks

TASK 201 - Preliminary hazard list. The first look at potential hazards. Some of the items on this list may later prove to be of little concern, and additional hazards will be considered as the program progresses.

Task 202 - Preliminary hazard analysis. Document in accordance with DI-SAFT-80101, System Safety Hazard Analysis Report. The format for the PHA may or may not be specified by the MA.

TASK 203 - Subsystem hazard analysis. Document in accordance with DI-SAFT-80101, System Safety Hazard Analsysis Report. The format needs to be the same for the prime and all subs, associates, etc. Usually a matrix format for reporting.

TASK 204 - System Hazard Analysis. Document as with SHA. Interface safety problems of subsystems that have been individually analyzed for safety.

TASK 205 - Operating and support hazard analysis. Document as with other hazard analyses. Covers environment, personnel and procedures.

TASK 206 - Occupational health hazard assessment. Document as with hazard analyses. Toxicity, hazardous materials and their waste, handling of hazardous items, protective clothing and devices. Document in accordance with DI-SAFT-80106.

TASK 207 - Safety verification. Were the requirements, specifications, standards, regulations and guidelines observed and met? Document with DI-SAFT-80102, System Safety Assessment Report.

TASK 208 - Training. How the training is to be performed and who is to be trained. Details are contained in the SSPP.

TASK 209 - Safety assessment. Use DI-SAFT-80102, Safety Assessment Report. Lists and discusses residual safety problems, special controls and procedures.

TASK 210 - Safety compliance assessment. Document with DI-SAFT-80102, Safety Assessment Report. Wrap-up verification of the safety status of the completed system. On a low-risk system, this may be the only analysis report.

TASK 211 - Safety review of ECPS and request for deviation/waiver. Document using DI-SAFT-80103 for Engineering Change Proposals and DI-SAFT-80104 for Waivers or Deviations. Correction of one problem may lead to other (even more serious) problems. The SOW must direct that the MA be notified if the change or deviation degrades the existing safety level.

TASK 212 - Software Safety Analysis. Documented as with other hazard analyses.

TASK 213 - GFE/GFP system safety analysis. Document as with hazard analyses. Analysis of government furnished equipment that directly interfaces with the contractor's equipment.

Contractor System Safety Organization

Different contractors have different system safety organizations. In some companies the system safety group may consist of a small number of people who act as "referees" on safety matters, with the actual hazard analyses being performed in the individual design areas. In other companies, the system safety group may be much larger with expertise in nearly all of the disciplines that are involved in the design. The latter type organization generally performs all of the hazard analyses within the system safety group. Neither of these two extremes are inherently better than the other, and the nature of the total system safety effort is usually a reflection of management interest and involvement.

Regardless of the type of system safety organization, there are several basic functions that are expected to be performed. The following is a listing of some of those functions which might be used to evaluate those performing a contracted system safety program, or used for a self-audit in an in-house program. All items may not apply to all activities, and with some experience, other items will be added.

Functions of a System Safety Organization

1. Ensure that the company safety policies are carried out by all personnel concerned.
2. Keep management informed on the safety program, its status, significant problems, deficiencies and methods of procedure.
3. Develop guidance by which the safety program will be carried out during the entire life cycle.
4. Review all safety requirements affecting the company product to ensure customer satisfaction. These requirements may be stated in contracts, specifications, standards, federal or state laws, federal regulations, e.g., Federal Transportation Commission Regulations, technical codes and good engineering practice. To focus attention on these safety requirements, the system safety organization must know their contents, implications and changes.
5. Review design, maintainability, reliability, production, test, quality assurance, logistics, human factors and training plans and criteria to ensure that there is a proper integration of safety activities into the product development.

6. Be cognizant of new processes, materials, equipment and information that might benefit the safety program.

7. Recommend these new safety developments that could be beneficial to the proper organization.

8. Analyze the product and its components to ensure that all hazards are eliminated or controlled to a degree acceptable by the MA. Recommend containment methods to minimize damage from uncontrolled hazards. Update analyses as development, testing and production proceed.

9. Review histories of hazards, failures and mishaps in existing systems to ensure that design deficiencies are not repeated in the new design or product.

10. Participate in design participation and reviews to ensure that incompatible or unsafe components, arrangements, subsystems or procedures are not incorporated.

11. Participate in trade-off studies.

12. Monitor failure and incident reports to determine discrepancies, deficiencies and/or trends that might affect safety. Make suitable recommendations for corrective action.

13. Prepare safety analyses required by the customer or his integrating contractor.

14. Develop safety analysis requirements, procedures and milestones to be observed by the subcontractors. Ensure that they understand all aspects of the safety program, the requirements imposed and how their data and analyses will be integrated into the total system safety effort.

15. Ensure that safety training programs are adequate to meet organizational needs. Initiate actions to improve these programs as necessary.

16. Determine whether detection and warning devices, protective equipment and/or emergency and rescue equipment are required for the system. Ensure that the equipment selected is suitable for the specific hazards that might be encountered.

17. Disseminate information on hazards to others.

18. Ensure that safety warning and caution notes are incorporated in procedures, checklists and manuals to warn the personnel of potential problems.

19. Maintain liaison with customer safety organizations, associate contractors, subcontractors, other suppliers, consultants and government safety agencies.

20. Serve on boards and committees dealing with industrial safety, bioenvironmental engineering, human engineering and related fields.

21. Develop investigation plans for any mishaps involving the product.

22. Ensure that corrective action is taken to prevent the recurrence of mishaps through the same, or similar, deficiencies or practices.

System Safety Checklist

The system safety checklist shown on the following pages is an approach to an evaluation list for rating a system safety program.

System Safety Checklist

Item	Adequate Yes	No	Remarks
1. System safety program plan and requirements documented as a contract exhibit.			
2. Contractor system safety tasks, task objectives, and reporting requirements defined for the applicable element of the life cycle.			
3. System safety in-process review schedule, and decision alternatives defined for each major decision point in the life cycle phase.			
4. System safety specification review and updating schedule established for specifications being generated.			
5. System safety participation scheduled for major design reviews in all life cycle phases.			
6. Approved data sources and analytical techniques for preliminary hazard analyses.			
7. System safety verification and evaluation test requirements defined.			
8. ECP safety review requirements and contractor procedures defined.			
9. System safety data requirements described in DID (DD 1664) and appended to safety requirements exhibit.			
10. System safety requirements defined and referenced to CDRL (DD 1423).			
11. Requirements for closed-loop failure data and accident report collection, analysis, feedback corrective action, and status reporting defined.			
12. Requirements and procedures defined for vendor/subcontractor safety programs.			
13. System safety participation schedule established for review and approval of procurement specifications.			

Item	Adequate Yes	No	Remarks
14. Requirements and procedures defined for explosives and hazardous materials management.			
15. Requirements for GFE safety evaluation defined.			
16. System safety test plan, test design criteria and acceptance requirements defined.			
17. System safety requirements defined for maintenance and production facilities.			
18. Explosive Safety Board presentations prepared.			
19. Provisions made for managing activity on-site review and evaluation of product.			
20. System safety requirements, including the establishment of a data bank, in accordance with DID's and CDRL's.			
21. Data submission schedule consistent with design program review schedule.			
22. Action addresses identified for each CDRL item.			
23. Clearly defined content, analysis procedures and format for data presentation.			
24. Operational conditions, mission profiles, environmental factors, performance characteristics, etc., defined.			
25. Design reviews, safety trade-offs and minimum acceptable safety requirements defined.			
26. Possible system safety interface problems defined.			
27. System safety tests, test conditions and success criteria for proof of conformance to the specified requirements defined.			
28. System safety analysis reports conform to review criteria.			
29. Subsystem and system hazard analyses, failure mode and effect analysis and feasibility studies validated.			

Item	Adequate		Remarks
	Yes	No	
30. System safety trade-offs with performance, feasibility and availability checked as realistic and practicable.			
31. System safety critical areas identified.			
32. Risks and man-rating requirements, limitations and other special areas of safety concern highlighted.			
33. Areas requiring additional investigations and system safety studies defined.			
34. Proposed corrective actions or preventative measures and design alternatives identified as practicable.			
35. Maintenance and logistics requirements and planning criteria consistent with system safety design requirements.			
36. Preliminary and final plans for maintenance and maintenance concepts compatible with system safety operational and support hazards analyses.			
37. Operator training and emergency procedures defined.			
38. Plans and schedules for formal review of ILS/system safety coordination and planning support established.			
39. Test requirements and planning exhibits include provisions for integrated system safety test and demonstration plans.			
40. Individual system safety test plans outlined to include objectives, procedures and data requirements.			
41. Preliminary test flow diagram for design/development/production consistent with overall program milestone schedule.			
42. Basic test requirements outlined, including acceptance demonstration, technical evaluation and operational evaluation.			
43. Range safety and range safety plan requirements established.			

Item	Adequate		Remarks
	Yes	No	
44. System safety analysis results summarized in packaging, handling, sportation analyses, technical documentation package and program master plan.			
45. Analysis techniques consistent through preliminary hazard analyses to operating and support hazard analyses.			
46. Analysis techniques of subcontractors consistent with those of the contractor.			
47. Risk management criteria established and documented.			
48. System safety inputs to operation and support publications established.			
49. Formal follow-up procedures for hazard actions defined.			
50. System safety program plan consistent with the system safety management plan.			

Figure 10.2. System Safety Checklist

Self-Study Questions

1. All information listed in the data item description *must* be reported by the contractor.
   - _____ a. True
   - _____ b. False

2. The statement of work is used to:
   - _____ a. Provide the contractor with general safety instructions
   - _____ b. Provide for data submittal
   - _____ c. Amplify and/or detail the requirements of MIL STD 882
   - _____ d. Describe how the contractor is planning to conduct safety

3. Data generated during a contract is presented to the managing activity:
   - _____ a. As required in the DID
   - _____ b. As soon as it is generated
   - _____ c. Upon his written or telephoned request
   - _____ d. Only if included in a CDRL

4. Although there may be some legal question, in general, proprietory data is:
   - _____ a. Data reported in accordance with a CDRL
   - _____ b. Data available to the managing activity at the contractor
   - _____ c. Non-specified data developed at the contractor's expense
   - _____ d. Data that the contractor has purchased elsewhere

5. Task 209 - System Safety Assessment is used to:
   - _____ a. Require the reporting of compliance with requirements
   - _____ b. Require a "wrap-up" report on the system safety program
   - _____ c. Measure the system safety performance of the contractor
   - _____ d. Require the reporting of safety assessments and levys

6. Tailoring of a system safety program is required in order to:
   - _____ a. Ensure an adequate level of system safety
   - _____ b. Prevent "over-safetying" of a program
   - _____ c. Make the system safety activity fit the program activity
   - _____ d. All of the above

7. The system safety program plan is prepared by:
   - _____ a. The managing activity
   - _____ b. The contractor
   - _____ c. The procuring activity
   - _____ d. The subcontractors

8. In order to maintain the highest level of system safety, system safety personnel should not participate in trade-off studies.

    _____ a. True

    _____ b. False

9. When a deviation from a contractual requirement is requested by the contractor, he must:

    _____ a. Increase the level of safety

    _____ b. Maintain the level of safety

    _____ c. Inform the MA if the level of safety is reduced

    _____ d. Pay for any safety changes

10. The CDRL should require the following safety data:

    _____ a. Only that necessary to validate the contractor's actions

    _____ b. All safety data

    _____ c. Only hazard category I data

    _____ d. Hazard category I and II data

11. The requirements of MIL STD 882:

    _____ a. Are required for contractor work, but not for "in-house"

    _____ b. Are never "echoed" in the statement of work

    _____ c. Are tailored to provide a cost effective program

    _____ d. Are all included in every contracted program

12. Task 208 - Training-has two aspects. These are:

    _____ a. Training designers and contractors

    _____ b. Training operators and support personnel

    _____ c. Training people and writing training plans

    _____ d. Training of specific contractor personnel and training for certification of test and operating personnel

13. The problem of hazardous materials falls under the cognizance of the Occupational Safety and Health Act is not addressed by system safety.

    _____ a. True

    _____ b. False

14. DI-SAFT-80100, the system safety program plan DID requires:

    _____ a. The identification of system safety milestones

    _____ b. The description of system operation procedures

    _____ c. The reporting of newly discovered hazards

    _____ d. A listing of identified hazards

15. The system safety program plan should contain:

    _____ a. A closed-loop hazard tracking procedure

    _____ b. A description of hazard analysis techniques

    _____ c. A description of interfaces with other safety disciplines

    _____ d. All of the above

11

Human Factors

Introduction

A *personnel subsystem* is defined in the *Handbook of Instructions for Aerospace Personnel Subsystem Designers*, (AFSCM 80-3]) as "That major part of a system which, through effective implementation of its various elements, provides the human performance necessary to operate, maintain and control the system in its intended environment."

And Willie Hammer in his *Handbook of System and Product Safety* adds, "In spite of his propensity for making errors and despite any desire to eliminate him from systems in which he can generate damage, man is still the most important single item in any system, no matter how complex."

Human Engineering General

To obtain maximum effectiveness in any system, the best capabilities of man-machine must be integrated. There are some tasks that can be best achieved by a machine, while others are more well-suited for a human being. The functions to be performed by personnel and hardware should be reviewed through suitable analyses.

Human Engineering Analysis Techniques

Several techniques have been developed to evaluate human engineering factors. Some of these are better suited for pre-design analysis while others are better suited for post-design analysis. An overview of a few of these techniques will be presented here.

Link Analysis

A *link analysis* is a means of evaluating transmission of information by type (visual, auditory, tactile), rate, load, and adequacy. The analysis is accomplished by examining the operational relationship between two units (two persons, or a person and a machine).

A *link* is a connection between two elements; an *element* is a person, control, display, piece of equipment or station. Link analysis attempts to reduce the lengths of the most important or most frequently used links at the expense of the less important or less frequently used links.

Links are rated by their use factor (frequency of employment) and importance (a ranking of the criticality of the action). Scales are rated from 1 to 5 or 1 to 10. The higher numbers indicate higher use/importance, and the lower numbers indicate infrequent, less important use.

The link analysis procedure follows:

1. Prepare a drawing indicating the location of the elements. If distance is a factor, the drawing should be to scale.
2. Draw links between the various stations.
3. Determine the frequency of the links.
   a) Count the number of times each task element is accomplished.
4. Establish the criticality of each link:
   a) Importance of the task
   b) Level of difficulty
   c) Need for speed and control by the performer
   d) Frequency with which the task must be accomplished
   e) Total time involved
5. Determine a criticality value for each link, using the product of the frequency and the importance factor.
6. Re-arrange the elements so that links with the highest end-use have the shortest links.
7. Consider "emergency" operations carefully. Avoid obscure and/or complicated links in an emergency situation.

Figure 11.1 (adapted from "Eye Movements of Aircraft Pilots During Instrument Landing Approaches" by Fitts, Jones and Milton, *Aeronautical Review*, February 1950), shows the results of a scanning motion picture camera which recorded the eye movements. A subsequent analysis of the movements derived the percentages shown in the figure. The frequency indicates the use factor, with all movements having some degree of criticality. (Movements comprising less than 2 percent of the total are not included.)

The figure demonstrates that the most frequent movement, between the cross-pointer and the directional gyro, required eye movement across another indicator. In fact, in 43 percent of the eye movements, another instrument had to be passed over during an eye shift. This would tend to indicate that a more efficient rearrangement of the indicators should be considered.

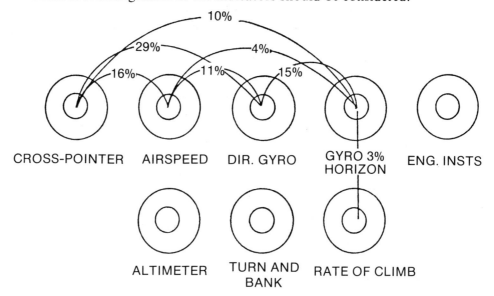

Figure 11.1. Link Analysis Diagram

Critical Incident Technique

In essence, the *critical incidence technique* may be considered an accident investigation where there has been *no* accident. This technique is based on collecting information on hazards, near misses, and unsafe conditions and practices from operationally experienced personnel.

It has been found that people are more willing to talk about "close calls" than about injury or damage accidents in which they were personally involved, the implication being that if no (reportable) loss ensued, no blame for the mishap would be forthcoming. (This also shows how smart they were to avoid the potential mishap!)

This technique is based on studies by Fitts and Jones, Wright-Patterson Air Force Base, circa 1947, and later by Tarrant of the Department of Labor. An example of this technique can to be found in interviews of Air Force pilots at the close of World War II on errors made in operating aircraft controls and reading instruments. Over 480 errors in control operations were reported, with over 80 percent of these being the result of design errors.

These errors were subclassified as:

Substitution errors	Confusing one switch with another, or failing to identify a control when it was needed.
Adjustment errors	Operating a control too fast or too slow; moving a switch to the wrong position; moving switches or controls out of the required sequence.
Forgetting errors	Failing to check, unlock or use a control at the proper time.
Reversal errors	Moving a control in the wrong direction.
Unintentional activation errors	Inadvertent operation of a control.
Unreachable control errors	Inability to reach a control, or problems resulting from "putting head in the cockpit" to reach a control that could not be otherwise reached.

A study by Stanford Research Institute found the following differences between "reports" and critical incident technique "interviews:"

Table 11.1
Frequency of Incidents (%)

	Reports	Interviews
Faulty design	1.9	21.7
Faulty construction	80.8	29.0
Faulty operation	17.3	49.3

Note that whereas the large majority of "causes" in the original reports were listed as "faulty construction," the critical incident interviews brought out the fact that nearly half of the incidents were really due to "faulty operation."

Critical Incident Techniques Procedures

Tarrant suggests the following procedure for carrying out a *critical incident technique* program:

1. A group of volunteers are given a list of typical incidents involving the system in question. The list stimulates recall.
2. Participants are asked to describe any incidents of which they have knowledge.
3. Questioning is continued until human errors or unsafe conditions can be described.

Attempts have been made to obtain this type of information from questionnaires alone, but the success level has been much lower than with the personal interviews.

Procedure (TASK) Analysis

The *procedure analysis* is a time-order review of the actions that must be performed, generally in relation to the mission task, the equipment that must be operated, and the environment in which the personnel must exist. This analysis determines the required tasks, exposure to hazards, criticality and procedural steps of each task, equipment characteristics, and mental and physical demands.

There are computer programs available that assist in the development of the tasking process and provide an analysis of the input tasks.

The safety type task analysis is performed to identify equipment, procedures and operations that could be dangerous to personnel, hardware and/or facilities during field activities or tests.

Safety task analyses are of three types:

1. Those used to evaluate system component characteristics, especially those that are inherently hazardous.
2. Those used to establish component or system reliability.
3. Those used to prove the procedures generated for field personnel.

Task analyses may also used to determine or to validate manning levels. Although this may not have a direct relationship to system safety, there may well be some indirect connection between manning level and the safety of the system.

Generalities

1. Any equipment or procedure that can be used incorrectly will someday be used incorrectly (Murphy's Law). One must consider the outcomes due to this in the Task Analysis.
2. No matter how simple a procedure may be, it should be examined for possibilities of error and danger.
3. Personnel tend to take shortcuts to avoid arduous, lengthy, uncomfortable or unintelligible procedures.
4. Most man-machine relationships involve procedural problems in the use of the equipment, rather than failures in the equipment.
5. All unnecessary steps should be eliminated, and critical steps must be accentuated.
6. Procedures requiring person-to-person communication should be kept to a minimum and should be as simple as possible.
7. Personnel are so knowledgeable, careful and adept that *they* will make no errors although they know that *others* may err! The ones who are the most self-assured must be specially protected.

Self-Study Questions

1. All functions are performed better and more efficiently by a machine.
   - _____ a. True
   - _____ b. False

2. A link analysis evaluated transmission of information by all of the following types except:
   - _____ a. Feel
   - _____ b. Sound
   - _____ c. Smell
   - _____ d. Sight

3. A critical incident technique analysis may be conducted most efficiently by:
   - _____ a. Use of a questionnaire
   - _____ b. Having the subject "fill in the blanks"
   - _____ c. Use of pre-prepared form /
   - _____ d. Use of verbal interview format

4. Task analyses for system safety purposes include the evaluation of procedures for:
   - _____ a. Operating personnel
   - _____ b. Production personnel
   - _____ c. Design personnel
   - _____ d. Engineering personnel

5. Personnel tend to take shortcuts to avoid:
   - _____ a. Simple tasks
   - _____ b. Lengthy tasks
   - _____ c. Concise tasks
   - _____ d. Short tasks

6. The critical incident technique process is usually valid for:
   - _____ a. Recall of accident information only
   - _____ b. Disclosure of events that happened to others
   - _____ c. Recall of near misses as well as mishaps
   - _____ d. Discussion of a theoretical occurrence

7. Relating of a link analysis should be based on:
   - _____ a. Importance of the task only
   - _____ b. Normal operations only
   - _____ c. Frequency only
   - _____ d. Level of difficulty

8. People are usually more willing to discuss their involvement with incidents that did not develop into a mishap.

    _____ a. True

    _____ b. False

9. A thorough procedure analysis will probably require:

    _____ a. The questioning of a large number of people

    _____ b. A computer program

    _____ c. A complete simulator of the proposed system

    _____ d. The use of interviews instead of a questionnaire

10. Most mishaps in a man-machine relationship are due to:

    _____ a. Material failures

    _____ b. Equipment breakdown

    _____ c. Procedural problems

    _____ d. Hardware selection

11. Procedures requiring person-to-person communication should:

    _____ a. Be kept as simple as possible

    _____ b. Require a specialized vocabulary

    _____ c. Be made on the "challenge/response" basis

    _____ d. Taped for possible accident investigation use

12. The critical incident technique is useful for developing:

    _____ a. "Lessons learned" where there are few accident statistics

    _____ b. The real causes of already documented accidents

    _____ c. Errors of ommission as well as of commission

    _____ d. All of the above

13. Simple procedures should also be examined for potential human factors problems.

    _____ a. True

    _____ b. False

14. To reduce personnel involvement in accidents:

    _____ a. Supervisory personnel must always be present

    _____ b. Critical steps should be accentuated

    _____ c. People should work in groups

    _____ d. All of the above

15. A task analysis can be used to validate manning levels.

    _____ a. True

    _____ b. False

12

Interfaces

Introduction

In the development of a weapons system, system safety does not stand alone. Not only do other disciplines depend on system safety for inputs, but system safety is greatly dependent on the outputs from other disciplines. Many of these associated disciplines are grouped under the name "ilities." We'll begin this chapter with an examination of some of these disciplines. Later in this chapter, we'll examine the interfaces between system safety and these disciplines.

Reliability - R

Reliability is the probability that the system (or some portion thereof) will perform its intended function for a specified period of time under a set of specified conditions. Reliability is usually expressed in terms of *mean time between failures* (MTBF), or in *failure rate* (λ).

$$R = e^{-\lambda t}$$

where λ is the failure rate = $1/MTBF$

For example, a device has a MTBF of 1,100 hours. The reliability during a 24 hour mission is 0.978.

$$R = e^{-(24/1100)} = 0.978$$

Survivability - S

Survivability is the measure of the degree to which a system (or portion thereof) will withstand the environment in which it is placed and not suffer abortive impairment of its ability to accomplish the designated mission. Both the operational and hostile environments are to be considered. The fundamental difference between reliability and survivability is that the former relates to activity carried out *prior* to the appearance of a failure or degradation in accordance with a *priori* standards, while the latter relates to activities conducted *subsequent* to the occurrence of a failure or degradation.

Maintainability - M

Maintainability is the probability that the system or some portion thereof will be retained in, or restored to, a specified condition within a given period of time, presuming that the maintenance is performed in accordance with a set of prescribed procedures and allocated resources. Maintainability is usually measured in the number of man-hours per flight (or per flight hour) required to maintain the system. This produces an index not amendable to other "probability-type" numbers.

Availability - A

Availability is a measure of the degree to which a system is ready for use. Three types of availability are defined:

1. *Inherent availability,* A_i - The probability that a system, when used under stated conditions, will operate satisfactorily at any given time.

$$A_i = MTBF / (MTBF + MTTR)$$
where   MTBF = Mean time between failures
              MTTR = Mean time to repair

2. *Achieved availability,* A_a - The probability that a system or equipment when used under stated conditions, in an *ideal support* environment, shall operate satisfactorily at any given time.

$$A_a = MTBM / (MTBM + M)$$
where   MTBM = Mean time between maintenance
            M   = Maintenance down time resulting from both preventative and corrective maintenance.

3. *Operational availability,* A_O - The probability that a system or equipment when used under stated conditions and in an *actual* supply environment shall operate satisfactorily at any given time.

$$A_O = MTBM / (MTBM + MDT)$$

where $\quad$ MDT = Mean down time, including supply down time.

Human Factors

To put it most simply, the *human factor* is the fitting of the machine to the man. Human factors can be quantified only by the development of relative scales such as the Cooper-Harper scale used in flight testing.

Quality Assurance - QA

Quality assurance is the planned, systematic set of actions taken to provide adequate confidence that the system, or some portion thereof, will perform satisfactorily when put to use. Quality is a relative term, so quality assurance becomes a matter of attempting to reach some desired level of accomplishment at a specified level of workmanship.

Value Engineering

Value engineering is the process of developing the maximum output for the least cost input, or the maximization of output utility to input cost relationship.

Systems Effectiveness

Systems effectiveness is an overall measure of the combined effects of all of the disciplines on the effectiveness of the system. Although there have been attempts to quantify a measure of effectiveness, no practical mathematical relationship has yet been developed.

Trade-Offs

Trade-offs are made to improve some characteristic of a system at a minimum cost to another characteristic. Changes in many of the "ilities" are interrelated. For example, an improvement in the maintainability of a system will usually improve the availability, and improved reliability reduces the need for maintenance actions. Figure 12.1 shows a typical relationship between maintainability, reliability and availability.

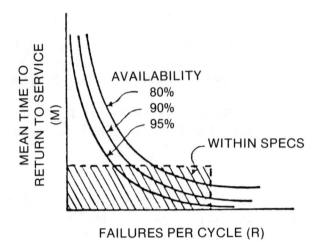

Figure 12.1. Trade-off diagram

Interfaces

Figure 12.2 shows (using acronyms that have been defined elsewhere) the interfaces between system safety and several other related activities, indicating what information is fed to the other disciplines by system safety and what information is furnished by these groups to system safety. Although system safety is shown as the core of these interfaces, system safety is not the center of the universe, and a similar diagram could be created with any of the other activities in the middle.

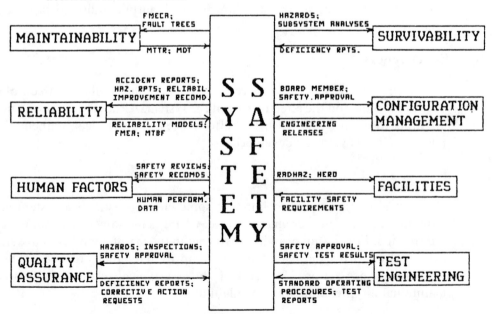

Figure 12.2. System safety interfaces

Self-Study Questions

1. The probability that a system may be restored to a specified condition in a given time is called:
   - _____ a. Maintainability
   - _____ b. Reliability
   - _____ c. Availability
   - _____ d. Survivability

2. Survivability has only to do with system maintenance in a wartime (hostile) environment.
   - _____ a. True
   - _____ b. False

3. The probability that a system will perform as specified for a given time is called:
   - _____ a. Maintainability
   - _____ b. Reliability
   - _____ c. Availability
   - _____ d. Survivability

4. The ability of a system to withstand some external influence is called:
   - _____ a. Maintainability
   - _____ b. Reliability
   - _____ c. Availability
   - _____ d. Survivability

5. Preventative maintenance is not considered in inherent availability.
   - _____ a. True
   - _____ b. False

6. Value engineering might be characterized as obtaining the maximum output:
   - _____ a. At the maximum cost
   - _____ b. At the minimum cost
   - _____ c. With the highest quality
   - _____ d. With adequate performance

7. Quality assurance is the obtaining of the maximum output:
   - _____ a. At the maximum cost
   - _____ b. At the minimum cost
   - _____ c. With the highest quality
   - _____ d. With adequate performance

8. A measure of all of the "ilities" is called:
   _____ a.   System effectiveness
   _____ b.   Operational availability
   _____ c.   Quality
   _____ d.   Value

9. The contractor's group that might get fault trees from a system safety group in order to provide for support operations to mitigate problem is:
   _____ a.   Reliability
   _____ b.   Human factors
   _____ c.   Maintainability
   _____ d.   Test engineering

10. Mean time between failures is the inverse of failure rate.
    _____ a.   True
    _____ b.   False

11. Failure data for use by system safety is usually obtained from the contractor's group:
    _____ a.   Reliability
    _____ b.   Human factors
    _____ c.   Maintainability
    _____ d.   Test engineering

12. Human factors is usually quantified by the use of:
    _____ a.   Probability functions
    _____ b.   Personnel failure rates
    _____ c.   Relative indices
    _____ d.   Maintenance workload data

13. Operational availability assumes a zero-time supply pipeline.
    _____ a.   True
    _____ b.   False

14. The principal difference between the reliability and system safety groups is that the latter is concerned only with:
    _____ a.   Hardware items
    _____ b.   Software problems
    _____ c.   Fail-safe occurrences
    _____ d.   Failures that result in damage/injury

15. A high mean time to return to service can still result in a high availability if:
    _____ a.   Failure rate is high
    _____ b.   Inherent availability is considered
    _____ c.   Reliability is low
    _____ d.   Failure rate is low

13

Testing

Introduction

System safety tests and verification are performed to provide confidence in the system safety analyses that have been performed. This is accomplished by performing hazard analyses, proposing corrective actions, and then performing hazard analyses of the proposed corrective actions. These corrective actions are then verified by an independent party prior to management review and approval, after which the design is incorporated. If there are questions as to the design, or if the design is adjudged to be safety critical, the design should be verified by safety tests. If these safety tests indicate further, continuing or new safety problems, additional hazard analyses are performed, these actions are verified, and the process continues.

Task 106 of the MIL STD requires that "...safety is considered in test and evaluation." This means both testing for safety and safety in testing.

Systems Engineering Tests

System engineering tests are performed during the full-scale development phase to provide empirical test data which can be used to generate design data information. This information may be difficult to obtain otherwise, due to the inadequacy of analytical methods and/or the difficulty of theoretical solutions.

The empirical data provided by tests are required at critical decision points and major decision milestones in the system life cycle. These data are used to verify early design decisions, to evaluate problem areas in given design parameters, and to demonstrate design conformance to specified safety requirements.

Test and Evaluation Master Plan (TEMP)

The *test and evaluation master plan* (TEMP) is required by DoD INST 5000.3 series as implemented for the Navy by OPNAV 3960.10. The TEMP is prepared prior to initiation of full-scale development to identify and integrate the effort and schedules of all testing and evaluation to be accomplished, and to ensure that testing and evaluation are completed prior to major decision points. For the Navy, approval of the Chief of Naval Operations is required for all TEMPS for *acquisition categories* (ACAT) I, II and III. (The test plan for ACAT IV is not called TEMP). The acquisition categories are determined by the cost of the research and development and/or production, with ACAT I being the most expensive.

The format for a TEMP (which is limited to no more than 30 pages) is as follows:

1. Description of the system
2 Integrated schedule
3. Developmental test and evaluation outline
4. Operational test and evaluation outline
5. Performance acceptance test and evaluation outline (if applicable)
6. Resource summary
7. References.

The TEMP should be reviewed annually and about two months prior to major decision points such as the JMRB.

Types of Tests and Evaluations

The *developmental test* (DT) (Army) or the *developmental test & evaluation* (DT&E) (Navy) is used to demonstrate that the engineering design and development is complete, that the design and safety risks have been minimized, that the systems will meet specifications, and that the system's military utility will be met when the system is introduced into the fleet. The principal purpose of developmental testing is to ensure that the system is designed and built in accordance with the specifications.

The *operational test* (DT) (Army) or the *operational test and evaluation* (OT&E) (Navy) is conducted to estimate the military utility of the proposed system, including operational effectiveness, operational suitability and the need for modifications. These tests provide the ultimate user with information on organization, personnel requirements, doctrine and tactics. The principal purpose of the operational tests is to ensure that the system meets the requirements of the user.

The *technical evaluation* (TECHEVAL) (Navy) is performed to investigate systems or equipment and to collect information to be used in answering technical questions. In the case of aircraft or missiles, the TECHEVAL will include the *Navy preliminary evaluation* (NPE), and/or the *Navy technical evaluation* (NTE)

In the Navy, the *operational evaluation* (OPEVAL) is conducted under the auspices of Commander, Operational Test and Evaluation Force (COMOPTEVFOR) with assistance from the development agency, as required, to determine the systems operability, maintainability and supportability by both qualitative and quantitative assessments. The conclusion of OPEVAL complete the *initial operational test and evaluation* (IOT&E) process.

Production acceptance test and evaluation (PAT&E) is conducted on production items to demonstrate that the items procured fulfill the requirements and specifications of the procurement contracts and agreements. PAT&E is conducted throughout the production phase.

The initial operational test & evaluation (IOT&E) is accomplished prior to commencement of the production phase to permit assessment of the operational effectiveness and suitability of the weapon system.

The *follow-on operational test and evaluation* (FOT&E) provides additional testing necessary for developing optimum procedures and tactics for both new and existing systems in the fleet. These tests are used to verify operational suitability of production units, and/or to confirm the correction of discrepancies previously disclosed. The FOT&E may also be used to develop requirements for future system development.

Board of Inspection and Survey (BIS/INSURV)

The *Board of Inspection and Survey* is the Navy's representative responsible for determining service acceptability. Acceptance trials for aircraft and missiles are conducted under sub-boards called BIS, while INSURV conducts the acceptance trials for ships.

Safety Test Requirements

In planning programs, consideration must be given to proper sequencing of tests to accommodate safety test requirements. Safety tests should be integrated with other tests, whenever possible, and for each test or series of tests, the test requirements should be specified to the test activity.

A test plan must be prepared that includes a statement of the test objectives and a description of the test conditions, test duration, and environmental conditions. It is essential that the objectives are definitive in regard to the factors to be evaluated. This includes a description of the specific safety tests and a listing of the data required. "Pass-Fail" criteria must be established *before* the testing is commenced.

All tests must be carried out in a safe manner. This is easier said than done because at times testing is more dangerous than actual operations, since the hazards introduced by testing conditions, instrumentation, etc. must be considered.

Safety Test Procedures

Test procedures should be prepared by the contractor and presented to the managing activity for approval at least 30 days prior to the test. These procedures should contain the following information:

1. Test management plan
   a) Identifies the activity having final responsibility for the proper conduct of the test.
   b) Covers the administrative procedures for resolving unforeseen technical difficulties and problems.
   c) States the pre-test requisites.
   d) Lists the safety precautions to be observed during the testing.
2. Step-by-step implementation
   a) Defines and identifies each step in the testing process
3. Data collection and data recording provisions
   a) Specify methods for manual and/or automatic collection and recording of data.
      (1) Include sample data forms.
      (2) Identify data for integrated tests so as to facilitate the analysis verification.
4. Instrumentation requirements
   a) Specify the instruments to be used.
   b) Certify that the instrumentation will not introduce hazards.

Test Reports

Test reports should contain an analysis and evaluation of the test for design guidance and should be prepared in a format usually stated in CDRL and/or DID. Each report should contain the following sections:

1. Test Objectives
   Statement of original objectives plus any revisions.

2. Test summary

   Summary of test results, conclusions and recommendations.
3. Test configuration

   Statement of the *actual* configuration and how this varies from the norm.
4. Test approach

   Description of how the test was to be conducted and how it was conducted.
5. Test set-up

   Description of test equipment instrumentation and facilities.
6. Test log

   Chronological test summary.
7. Test summary

   Detailed discussion of test results (identified to each test objective) with computational and analytical data to support the conclusions.
8. Recommend corrective action

   Design changes, safety devices, personnel training, etc.

Hazardous Tests

In conducting hazardous tests, the following significant precautions should be taken:

- Test personnel and electrically initiated ordnance are protected against hazardous levels of electromagnetic radiation.
- Explosives are not exposed during handling, storage and transport to those environments that could cause inadvertent initiation.
- Test personnel are protected against dangerous high voltages.
- Unauthorized personnel are restricted from hazardous areas.
- Test personnel are protected against injurious chemical agents.
- Adequate training concerning hazards is given to all test personnel.
- First aid and hospital facilities are available to treat injured personnel.
- The possibility of a catastrophe occurring in the test facility would not endanger lives of the public.
- Environments produced by the tests are not in conflict with the Environmental Policy Act (NEPA), Noise Control Act of 1972 and Toxic Substances Control Act of 1972.

Ordnance Safety Tests

The following are typical tests conducted on ordnance materials:

- Electrostatic discharge test
- Hazards of electromagnetic radiation to ordnance (HERO)

- 40-foot drop test
- Vibration test
- Temperature and humidity test for aggravated environment
- Cook-off test (enveloping flame)
- Cook-off test (slow heating)
- Catapult and arrested landing test
- Frequent impact test (high impact, small fragments)
- Separation from aircraft on landing test

Self-Study Questions

1. The tests conducted on items coming off the assembly to ensure that all of the procurement requirements and specifications are met are called:
   - _____ a. Technical evaluation
   - _____ b. Production acceptance tests
   - _____ c. Developmental tests
   - _____ d. Operational tests

2. The military worth of a new system is determined through:
   - _____ a. Technical evaluation
   - _____ b. Production acceptance tests
   - _____ c. Developmental tests
   - _____ d. Operational tests

3. Testing for safety must be accomplished prior to all other tests.
   - _____ a. True
   - _____ b. False

4. Determining if the system has been designed to meet the requirements is accomplished by:
   - _____ a. Technical evaluation
   - _____ b. Production-acceptance tests
   - _____ c. Developmental tests
   - _____ d. Operational tests

5. Initial operational test and evaluation is performed:
   - _____ a. Prior to the commencement of the production phase
   - _____ b. Prior to the commencement of full-scale engineering
   - _____ c. On the first production article
   - _____ d. On selected articles throughout production

6. In the early part of the life cycle, information is gathered to answer engineering problems with:
   - _____ a. Technical evaluation
   - _____ b. Production acceptance tests

_____ c.   Developmental tests
_____ d.   Operational tests

7.   A TEMP must be prepared for:
   _____ a.   All testing
   _____ b.   All acquisition category IV testing
   _____ c.   ACAT II testing
   _____ d.   Production acceptance testing only

8.   Operational tests are performed to ensure that the system meets the requirements of the user.
   _____ a.   True
   _____ b.   False

9.   A system safety test plan should contain:
   _____ a.   A summary of test results
   _____ b.   A statement of test objectives
   _____ c.   The test configuration
   _____ d.   A test log

10.   Pass-fail criteria for a test should be determined:
   _____ a.   After initial testing
   _____ b.   After final testing
   _____ c.   Before the test summary
   _____ d.   Before the start of testing

11.   Test sites should be limited to only those specifically authorized to participate in the testing.
   _____ a.   True
   _____ b.   False

12.   Testing for the effect of heat on a system should include:
   _____ a.   Fast temperature application only (direct flame)
   _____ b.   Slow temperature application only (slow heating)
   _____ c.   Indirect heating
   _____ d.   Both direct flame and slow heating tests

13.   Frequent impact tests on ordnance generally involve:
   _____ a.   High impact, large fragments
   _____ b.   Moderate impact, large fragments
   _____ c.   Moderate impact, small fragments
   _____ d.   High impact, small fragments

14. The activity having the final responsibility for a test is identified in:
    _____ a.   The test summary
    _____ b.   The test management plan
    _____ c.   The statement of work
    _____ d.   The test objectives

15. The test configuration should list the actual configuration, as well as:
    _____ a.   How this varies from the norm
    _____ b.   Who authorized any variation
    _____ c.   A statement that this is the standard configuration
    _____ d.   The precautions with the standard configuration

14

Mini System Safety (MISS) Program

Introduction

Military Standard 882B, System Safety Program Requirements, establishes procedures and tasks for the engineering and management of system safety programs. By tailoring these requirements, one is able to develop a system safety program that accommodates any size project.

A need however exists for the further delineation of a set of recommended procedures for conducting a small system safety program. Such a program may be called for small projects (e.g., the design and fabrication of a missile transport cart); projects with obviously minimal hazards (e.g., development of a new mechanical typewriter); projects that do not fit into the normal life cycle process (e.g., military facilities design and construction); and, unfortunately, projects for which the safety activity is dollar limited. A program to fill this need is presented here as a *mini-system-safety* (MISS) program.

Miss Actions

The following are recommended as a minimum effort in a system safety program:

*1. Prepare a preliminary hazards list (PHL)
*2. Conduct a preliminary hazard analysis (PHA)
*3. Assign a risk assessment code (RAC) for each item.
 4. Assign a priority for taking the recommended action to eliminate or control the hazards, according to the risk assessment codes.
 5. Evaluate the possibility of deleterious effects from interfaces between the recommended actions and other portions of the system.
 6. Take the recommended actions to modify the system.
*7. Prepare a system safety assessment report as a wrap-up of the system safety program.

The items denoted with an asterisk will be reviewed in some detail in the following sections.

Preliminary Hazards List (PHL)

The PHL can be derived in several ways. One of these is by examining the energy transfer in the system. This is based on the concept that all losses are created by an interference with the normal exchange of energy. The system is examined for incorrect, untimely or omitted energy exchanges as a base for the PHL. There are also available hazard review checklists in which hazards are listed, together with the usual occurrence mode, the possible cause and the possible effects.

A sample of such a list included by Hammer in his *Handbook of System and Product Safety* appears below:

HAZARD   - Toxicity
OCCURRENCE   - Any substance whose presence in relatively small amounts will produce physiological damage or disturbance.
                     - Any situation where a lack of oxygen for breathing may exist.
                     - Polluted atmosphere, especially in terrain depressed below its surroundings, or during a temperature inversion, or both.
POSSIBLE CAUSE   - Toxic gases or liquids. Fine metal or other particulate matter.
                     - Inadequate oxygen for respiration due to:
                       • High altitude
                       • Dilution by inert gases
                       • Oxygen consuming combustion
                     - Insufficient ventilation in occupied, enclosed spaces.
                     - Atmospheric pollution by industrial, automobile or other exhausts.
                     - Lack of respiratory protection.

	- Lack of skin protection.

POSSIBLE EFFECT
- Lack of skin protection.
- Inadequate personal cleanliness.
- Ingestion of toxic or contaminated materials or food.
- Outgassing of gases at low pressures in confined spaces.
- Irritation of eyes, nose, throat or respiratory passages.
- Damage to:
  - Respiratory system
  - Blood system
  - Body organs
  - Skin damage (dermatitis)
- Effects on nervous system (narcosis, anesthesia, paralysis, nerve damage).
- Annoyance or nausea caused by foul odors.
- Reduction in personnel efficiency or capabilities.
- Destruction of vegetation ....

And, as has been stated previously, one of the best sources for a preliminary hazards list is from past accident/incident reports and from operators and supporters of similar systems.

Preliminary Hazard Analysis

The *preliminary hazard analysis* (PHA) is the initial development of the relationships between hazard causes (faults), hazard effects and the recommended actions that could be taken to eliminate or control the hazards.

An in-depth hazard analysis generally follows the preliminary hazard analysis with a *subsystem hazard analysis* (SSHA), a *system hazard analysis* (SHA) and an *operating and support hazard analysis* (O&SHA), as appropriate. For a small safety program, the PHA will usually suffice as the only formal analysis.

Hazard (Fault)

The hazard should be explicitly described. That is to say, describe *where* the hazard is located (the sub-system, component or part) and the *mode of the hazard* (e.g., failed closed). This caution is necessary because a given hazard may have several modes of failure/missaction.

The hazard is usually listed by the sub-system component (e.g., winch brake) and the fault (e.g., fails unlocked).

Effect

Examine each fault to ensure that all of the effects are listed. Some hazards produce multiple effects and the most obvious effect may not be the most critical effect.

The effect should be unambiguous so that anyone reading the PHA can understand just what the problem is.

Hazard Severity

MIL STD 882B lists four (4) categories of hazard severity. The definitions for these categories may not be specific enough for a small system, so additional clarifying definitions may have to be added to relate the severity to specific injury classifications and specific damage limits (e.g., cost to repair). Although these are a modification of the MIL STD definitions, they should still fall within the MIL STD limits to avoid confusion.

Table 14.1 shows a typical modication of the hazard severity categories.

Table 14.1
Modification Hazard Severity Categories

CATEGORY	MIL STD 882B DEFINITION	ADDITIONAL DEFINITION
	CATASTROPHIC	
I	Death or system loss.	*Death or system loss.*
	CRITICAL	
II	Severe injury, severe occupational illness, or major system damage.	*Loss of an arm or leg, total disability, any hospitalization for an excess of 4 weeks. System damage in excess of $500,000.*
	MARGINAL	
III	Minor injury, minor occupational illness, or minor system damage.	*Injury less than that of Category II, but requiring more than first aid. Damage less than that of Category II, but more than $1,000.*
	NEGLIGIBLE	
IV	Less than minor injury, minor occupational illness or minor system damage.	*Injury requiring first aid or less. Material damage less than $1,000.*

Hazard Probability

The likelihood of occurrence of the undesired event can be expressed either relativistically or probabilistically. Unless one is dealing only with individual mechanical or electrical components, it is most likely that any preliminary hazard analysis will be relativistic in nature.

MIL STD 882B also presents a hazard probability listing and, as with the hazard severity listing, additional definitions may have to be furnished for small programs. Table 14-2 is a typical modification of the relativistic hazard probability scale from the MIL STD.

Table 14.2
Modification of Relativistic Hazard Probability Scale

RATING	MIL STD DEFINITION	ADDITIONAL DEFINITION
	FREQUENT	
A	Likely to occur frequently	*Likely to occur at least once during every evolution*
	PROBABLE	
B	Will occur several times in the life of an item	*Likely to occur at least once in every 10 evolutions*
	OCCASIONAL	
C	Likely to occur sometime in the program	*Likely to occur at least once during the life of the system*
	REMOTE	
D	Unlikely, but will possibly occur in the life of an item	*Remotely possible to occur during the entire program*
	IMPROBABLE	
E	So unlikely, it can be assumed such an occurrence may not be experienced.	*Probability of occurrence near zero*

Risk Assessment Codes

A risk assessment is a means for determining the rationale for the management of risks discovered during a hazard analysis. The early decisions in a system safety program are usually based on hazard severity alone because this is the only information available to the analyst. Then, as the analysis progresses, some determination as to hazard probability can be made and this must also be considered in the assessment of risks. With the two variables, severity and probability, it is common to develop a risk matrix so that the severity and probability inputs can define some *risk assessment code* (RAC) output. A typical risk assessment based on weighted relationships between severity and mishap probability is shown in figure 14.1.

HAZARD SEVERITY	MISHAP PROBABILITY			
	A LIKELY TO OCCUR IMMEDIATELY	**B** PROBABLY WILL OCCUR IN TIME	**C** MAY OCCUR IN TIME	**D** UNLIKELY TO OCCUR
I CATASTROPHIC — MAY CAUSE DEATH OR SYSTEM LOSS	1 (IMMINENT DANGER)	1 RISK ASSESSMENT CODE	2	3
II CRITICAL — MAY CAUSE SEVERE INJURY OR DAMAGE	1	2	3	4
III MARGINAL — MAY CAUSE MINOR INJURY OR DAMAGE	2	3	4	5
IV NEGLIGIBLE — PROBABLY WILL NOT AFFECT SAFETY	5	5	5	5

Figure 14.1. Risk assessment matrix.

Action Priority

Despite arguments in favor of and against the use of numerical system safety analyses, a ranking of some sort must be generally made of proposed actions, to indicate hazard criticality so that a management decision can be made as to where to concentrate effort and resources. Such a decision is facilitated by use of the risk assessment codes. Table 14.3 shows a typical use of RAC's to make broad safety management decisions.

Table 14.3
Hazard criticality ranked by risk assessment codes

RAC   ACTION

1   Elimination or positive control of the fault causing this hazard is imperative.

2   Elimination or positive control of the fault causing this hazard is highly desirable.

3   If the fault producing this hazard cannot be eliminated, some control over the effect should be exercised.

4   Minimal effort should be expended on the elimination or control of the fault causing this hazard.

5   No effort need be expended on correcting this fault.

Recommended Action

The ultimate purpose of any hazard analysis is to recommend corrective action that will eliminate or control the hazard. In order to accomplish this end, not only must the recommended action be the most efficient means of mitigating the hazard, but it must also be written in unambiguous terms so that others may understand what is proposed.

System Safety Assessment Report

The final wrap-up of the mini system safety program is the preparation of the *system safety assessment report* (SAR). This report is a comprehensive evaluation of the safety risks being assumed prior to test or evaluation of the system or at contract completion. It identifies all safety features of the hardware and system design, procedural hazards that may be present in the system being acquired, and specific procedural controls and precautions that should be followed.

Preparation instructions for the safety assessment report may be modified from those described in the data item description (DID) by means of DD Form 1423, Contract Data Requirement List (CDRL).

The safety assessment report is used to summarize and/or supplement the hazard analyses obtained and/or reported under the aegis of other DID's, but for small programs, this report may be the only documentation of the system safety program.

An outline of the safety assessment report follows:

1. Introduction - State the purpose of the safety assessment report.
2. System description - (May be developed by referencing other program documentation such as technical manuals, system safety program plan, etc.)
   a) State purpose and intended use of system.
   b) Provide brief historical summary of system development.
   c) Include a brief description of the system and its components. Include name, type, model number and general physical characteristics.
   d) As applicable, describe any other system(s) which will be tested or operated in combination with this system.
   e) As applicable, provide either photos, charts, flow/functional diagrams, sketches or schematics to support the system description, test or operation.
3. System operations
   a) Briefly describe or reference the procedures for operating the system. Discuss the safety features and control incorporated into the system as they relate to the operating procedures.
   b) Describe any special operating procedures needed to assure safe operations, including emergency procedures.

c) Describe anticipated operating environments and any special skills required for safe operation, maintenance or disposal.

d) Describe any special facility requirements or personal equipment to support the system

4. System safety engineering

a) Briefly summarize or reference the safety criteria and methodology used to classify and rank hazardous conditions.

b) Describe or reference analyses and tests performed to identify hazardous conditions inherent in the system.

(1) List all hazards that have been identified and considered from the inception of the program in an appendix to the safety assessment report. Discuss the hazards and the actions that have been taken to eliminate or control these hazards. Discuss the effects of potential hazards on probability of occurrence and severity level if contractually required.

(2) Discuss or reference results of tests conducted to validate safety criteria requirements and analyses.

5. Conclusions and recommendations

a) Include a short abstract of the results of the safety program efforts. Include a list of all significant hazards along with specific recommendations or precautions required to ensure the safety of personnel and property. Categorize the list of hazards as to whether or not they may be expected under normal or abnormal operating conditions.

b) If the system does not contain or generate hazardous materials (explosive, toxic, radioactive, carcinogenic, etc.) include a statement to that effect. For all hazardous materials generated or used in the system, include the following information:

(1) Material identification as to type, quantity and potential hazards.

(2) Safety precautions and procedures necessary during use, storage, transportation and disposal.

(3) A copy of the Material Safety Data Sheet (OSHA Form 20 or DD Form 1813) to satisfy specified requirements.

c) Conclude with a signed statement that all identified hazards have been eliminated or controlled, and that the system is ready to test or operate or proceed to the next acquisition phase. In addition, the contractor shall make recommendations applicable to the safe interface of his system with other system(s), as contractually required.

If a full safety assessment report is not required, it is recommended that, as a minimun, the report for the MISS program be structured as shown in table 14.4.

Table 14.4
Report for the MISS Program

- List of unresolved significant hazards
- List of special safety operating procedures
- List of safety emergency procedures
- List of safety-related facility requirements
- List of possible safety interfaces with other systems
- Statement of hazardous materials

The material included in table 14.4 may be expanded, as desired, by the addition of a listing of *resolved* significant hazards, and/or a brief description of the rationale for hazard classification and ranking.

Conclusion

Remember that the hazards encountered in a small program can be as severe as those of a major program and are as likely to occur. Usually one can expect fewer hazards in a small program. Caution needs to be exerted to ensure that in tailoring the system safety effort to fit a small program, one does not perform a wholesale slashing, but instead uses the tailoring process to obtain the optimum safety in the optimum system.

Self-Study Questions

1. The purpose of a MISS Program is:
   - _____ a. To develop a program that accommodates any size project
   - _____ b. To offer a less stringent program for safer systems
   - _____ c. To reduce the contractor's paperwork
   - _____ d. To accommodate a rush priority program

2. A system safety assessment report is:
   - _____ a. A final wrap-up of a MISS program
   - _____ b. A comprehensive evaluation of the safety risks
   - _____ c. A document identifying hardware safety features
   - _____ d. All of the above

3. A risk assessment code is based on:
   - _____ a. Recommended corrective action
   - _____ b. The likelihood of occurrence
   - _____ c. Weighted hazard severity/probability relationships
   - _____ d. Relationships between hazard causes and effects

4. The first recommended action in a MISS Program is to:

_____ a. Assign risk assessment codes

_____ b. Prepare a system safety assessment report

_____ c. Prepare a preliminary hazards list

_____ d. Conduct a preliminary hazard analysis

5. The MISS Program is recommended for small programs or those with minimal safety problems.

_____ a. True

_____ b. False

6. The ultimate purpose of any hazard analysis is to:

_____ a. Change the system

_____ b. Do another contract

_____ c. Recommend corrective actions

_____ d. All of the above

7. The program of MIL STD 882 must be used in their entirety unless otherwise approved by DoD.

_____ a. True

_____ b. False

8. The MISS Program is designed for:

_____ a. The development of a new missile design

_____ b. A project that doesn't fit into the normal life cycle phase

_____ c. Development of a system with high-level national exposure

_____ d. Development of a high-risk system

9. A risk assessment code of 4 (figure 14.1) indicates:

_____ a. The fault does not need to be fixed

_____ b. No money should be expended on this fault

_____ c. The fault should be fixed only after all others

_____ d. No special effort should be expended on this fault

10. A system safety assessment report should contain:

_____ a. The criteria used to rate the hazards

_____ b. A list of all hazards encountered

_____ c. A list of all frequency "A" hazards

_____ d. A list of all Category IV hazards

11. If a full system safety assessment report is not used, small programs should at least include in the project summary:

_____ a. A hazardous materials statement

_____ b. A list of safety related facility interfaces

_____ c.   A list of unresolved significant hazards

_____ d.   All of the above

12. The description of the system operation in a system safety assessment report must stand alone as a full and complete description.

   _____ a. True

   _____ b. False

13. The risk assessment codes are:

   _____ a. A firm statement for hazard elimination/control

   _____ b. A legal statement as to the hazards encountered

   _____ c. A management decision tool

   _____ d. The only basis for hazard elimination priority

14. The preliminary hazards list:

   _____ a. May contain entries that are not significant hazards

   _____ b. Is based only on previous mishaps

   _____ c. Contains hazard effects and recommended actions

   _____ d. Includes hazard severity classifications

15. The safety problems for a small project:

   _____ a. Can be as severe as for a major project

   _____ b. Are usually proportional to the size of the program

   _____ c. Are more likely to occur than those of a major program

   _____ d. Cost less to fix

15

Sample Problem

Introduction

To illustrate the procedures of a system safety program, a sample problem will be presented to offer some "almost hands-on" experience in conducting a system safety analysis.

The Project

A program is being established to develop and produce a gasoline-powered lawn mower for the consumer market in another country. This country has no federal regulations concerning safety, but the manufacturer desires to produce as safe a product as possible.

The mower will be powered by a one-and-a-half horsepower internal combustion engine with a pull-rope recoil starter. The machine will be self-propelled, forward and backward, at the operator's command. The machine will be fitted with a bag to catch the cuttings, but the mower may be operated without the bag. The retail price for the mower will be approximately $225.00 in U. S. currency.

Part I

Preliminary Hazards List

One of the first steps in the pre-design safety analysis is the development of a *preliminary hazards list* (PHL). The PHL is prepared in order to develop inputs to the preliminary hazard analysis, and is a listing, by sub-systems, of potential faults or hazards. At this time no consideration need be given to either the seriousness or the likelihood of occurrence of the faults. At the earliest stages, only sketchy information is available and one is usually limited to listing generic hazards, usually obtained from lessons learned from previous experiences with similar systems. As the analyst gains more expertise, "trivial" hazards will not even be listed as some degree of "mental" hazard analysis is accomplished.

The items in this list come from many sources, including company test data, company field-service reported failure data, consumer letters to the company, and industry lists of hazard causes.

As the design of the new lawn mower progresses, other hazards are added to this list and a full documentation is maintained so that an expanded list will be available for the next design.

The preliminary hazard list for this system may be developed as a subsystem and the fault associated with that subsystem that can cause a safety problem, as shown in table 15.1.

Table 15.1
Preliminary Hazards List

SUB-SYSTEM	FAULT
Engine, Fuel	Fuel line leak on hot engine exhaust manifold.

Task I

Develop a preliminary hazards list for the self-propelled lawnmower.

Self-Propelled Lawnmower

Preliminary Hazards List

SUBSYSTEM   FAULT

---------------------------------   ---------------------------------

---------------------------------   ---------------------------------

---------------------------------   ---------------------------------

---------------------------------   ---------------------------------

---------------------------------   ---------------------------------

---------------------------------   ---------------------------------

---------------------------------   ---------------------------------

---------------------------------   ---------------------------------

Part II

Additional Definitions

Before the hazard analysis is commenced, it would be well to provide additional definitions for both hazard severity and hazard probability in order to "fine tune" the analysis.

Hazard Severity

A dollar amount for material damage might be determined for each hazard category based on standard repair costs. A modified hazard severity chart may appear as shown in Table 15.2.

Table 15.2
Modified Hazard Severity Chart

Category	MIL STD 882B Definition	Additional Definition
	CATASTROPHIC	
I	Death or system loss.	Death or system loss. Repair cost greater than $150.00.

CRITICAL

| II | Severe injury, severe occupational illness, or major system damage. | Loss of eye, arm or leg; total disability, any hospitalization for an excess of 4 weeks. Repair cost less than $150.00, but greater than $75.00. |

MARGINAL

| III | Minor injury, minor occupational illness, or minor system damage. | Injury less than that of Category II, but requiring more than first aid. Repair cost less than $75.00, but more than $25.00. |

NEGLIGIBLE

| IV | Less than minor injury, minor occupational illness or minor system damage. | Injury requiring first aid or less. Repair cost less than $25.00. |

Hazard Probability

For large production quantities, the likelihood of occurrence is usually estimated both for a single unit and for the entire production. This is important in the consideration of risk, since a mishap involving a single user is a major event for the user, while one or two mishaps in an inventory of hundreds of thousands may not be much of a risk from the manufacturer's point of view. Additional definitions for both the consumer unit and the inventory are shown in table 15.3.

Table 15.3
Consumer unit and inventory definitions

Rating	MILSTD Definition	Additional Definition	
		Unit	Inventory
		FREQUENT	
A	Likely to occur frequently	Likely to occur at least once during every evolution	Likely to occur several times a day
		PROBABLE	
B	Will occur several times in the life of an item	Likely to occur several times in the life of the product	Likely to occur at least daily

		OCCASIONAL	
C	Likely to occur sometime in the life of an item	Likely to occur at least once during life of the product	Likely to occur at least once every 6 months
		REMOTE	
D	Unlikely, but remotely possible	Remotely possible to occur in the product life	Likely to occur at least once a year
		IMPROBABLE	
E	So unlikely, it can be assumed occurrence may not happen	Probability of occurrence near zero	Likely to occur only once or twice in the life of the product line

Preliminary Hazard Analysis

With the additional definitions for severity and probability and the preliminary hazards list, the preliminary hazard analysis can now be performed, using the following sequence of events:

1. For each sub-system/fault, determine the effect that this hazard will have on (a) the equipment and (b) the personnel who operate the equipment. It is quite possible that one fault may result in more than one effect, so give careful thought to including *all* of the possible outcomes.

2. Using the modified hazard category scale, rate each effect as to the *worst possible outcome.*

3. Using the modified hazard probability scale, rate each effect as to the most probable frequency of occurrence, using either the definition for consumer unit or for entire unit likelihood, whichever gives the clearer understanding of how often one can expect this effect to occur.

Task II

Using the preliminary hazard form shown in figure 15 i, prepare a PHA for the lawnmower through the hazard severity and hazard probability columns.

Sub-System Fault	Effect	Hza Sev	Haz Prob	Risk Code	Recommended Action

Figure 15.1. Preliminary hazard analysis form.

Part III

Task III

Using the risk assessment code, figure 15.2, assign a RAC to each event, based on the hazard severity and probability.

MISHAP PROBABILITY

HAZARD SEVERITY		A LIKELY TO OCCUR IMMEDIATELY	B PROBABLY WILL OCCUR IN TIME	C MAY OCCUR IN TIME	D UNLIKELY TO OCCUR
	I CATASTROPHIC MAY CAUSE DEATH OR SYSTEM LOSS	1 IMMINENT	1 RISK ASSESSMENT CODE	2	3
	II CRITICAL MAY CAUSE SEVERE INJURY OR DAMAGE	DANGER 1	2	3	4
	III MARGINAL MAY CAUSE MINOR INJURY OR DAMAGE	2	3	4	5
	IV NEGLIGIBLE PROBABLY WILL NOT AFFECT SAFETY	5	5	5	5

Figure 15.2. Risk assessment matrix.

Enter the RAC on the preliminary hazard analysis form.

Part IV

Recommended Action

For each effect, actions must be recommended to eliminate or mitigate the effect. The precedence on the actions should be:
1. Eliminate the hazard by design.
2. Control the effect of the hazard by design.
3. Control the effect by changing procedures.
4. Alert the user by cautions or warnings.

Task IV

Assign recommended actions for each item, and enter the actions on the preliminary hazard analysis form.

Part V

System Safety Assessment Report

Although this is not a government project, and has no mandated MIL STD 882 requirements, it is still worthwhile to prepare a system safety assessment report. As a very minimum this report should contain the following:

      a.A copy of the preliminary hazards list

b.   A copy of the preliminary hazard analysis

c.   A list of category I and II items that are unresolved

d.   A list of any "unique" or first-time solutions to safety problems developed during this project.

Task V

      List any unresolved category I or category II items.

Self-Study Questions

I. At a pre-design meeting, the following hazards were discussed. These were derived from reported mishaps, test analyses and general engineering observations. As the design progresses, additional hazards will be added to this list and analysis may show that some of these items are not very hazardous.

Item	Sub-System	Fault
1	Starter	"Snap back" during start
2	Starter	Rope breaks during starting pull
3	Starter	Fails to disengage after start
4	Cutter Blade	Comes off shaft while running
5	Cutter Blade	Fractures while engine is running
6	Powered Wheels	Wheels fail to stop when commanded
7	Powered Wheels	Wheels turn opposite to command
8	Powered Wheels	Wheels engage without command
9	Grass Exhaust	System clogs with grass cuttings
10	Grass Exhaust	Debris thrown directly out exhaust
11	Engine, Fuel	Fuel line leak on hot manifold
12	Engine, Exhaust	High decibel exhaust noise
13	Engine, Exhaust	Excessive smoke from exhaust

II. At the first analysis session, a negative utility in terms of *maximum* credible damage cost and/or personnel injury was assigned to each item.

Item	Damage/Injury	Negative Utility
1	Broken arm	More than first aid, but no hospitalization
2	Broken arm	More than first aid, but no hospitalization
3	Starter mechanism fractured	$50.00 repair bill
4	Damage to mower case	$70.00 repair bill
5	Loss of blade	$27.00 repair bill
		Personnel injury, severe lacerations with 5 weeks in hospital
6	Dented mower case	$20.00 repair bill
		Injury to bystander, loss of foot
7	Impact damage to mower	$100.00 repair bill
		Injury to operator; more than first aid, but hospitalization less than 3 weeks
8	Impact damage to mower	$100.00 repair bill
		Personnel injury to bystander
		Loss of limb

9	Injury to operator	Loss of hand while clearing debris
10	Injury to personnel	Loss of eye or head injury
11	Fire damage from leak	Loss of mower due to fire
12	Ear injury	Total loss of hearing
13	Eye injury	More than first aid, but no hospitalization

III. Continuing with the hazard analysis, a likelihood of occurrence was assigned to each item based on previous experience and reasonable forecasts.

Item	Likelihood
1	No more than once or twice per owner
2	No more than once or twice per owner
3	No more than once or twice per owner
4	Five or ten times per owner
5	Five or ten times per owner
6	Five or ten times per owner
7	Five or ten times per owner
8	No more than once or twice per owner
9	At least once every time mower is used
10	At least once every time mower is used
11	At least once every time mower is used
12	Five or ten times per owner
13	No more than once or twice per owner

Requirements

A. Prepare a preliminary hazard analysis (PHA) (Page 000) showing:
1. Sub-system/fault
2. Effect
3. Hazard severity (Table 15.2)
4. Hazard probability (Table 15.3)
5. Risk assessment code (figure 15.2)
6. Recommended actions (See Part IV, Page 000)

B. List all RAC 1 items

C. List all hazard severity I items

D. List any items whose hazard has been "controlled" by warnings or cautions

Index

More Books from Weber Systems, Inc.

Introduction to Linear Systems Analysis
by George M. Swisher

Designed as a textbook for use in senior and beginning graduate-level courses, this book is a sound introduction to linear systems theory for both discrete and continuous systems. As a balanced approach, classical techniques utilizing Laplace and Z transformations are covered as well as modern state space methods. Digital simulation is presented as an alternative to the analytical solutions. Topics covered include: stand-time systems; matrices, linear spaces, and linear operators; analysis of state equations for continuous and discrete time problems; system controllability, observation and stability, and design of linear feedback systems. A solutions manual is available.

Price U.S. $62.95   Canada $72.95
0-916460-05-3, 444 pp./133 illus., 6" x 9" hardcover

Linear Network Theory
by Norman Balabanian and Theodore Bickart

This book provides a comprehensive and careful development of linear network theory on a linear graph theory base, utilizing matrix-vector formulations of analytical methods. Both analysis and synthesis are treated, including an extended chapter on contemporary methods of active-RC synthesis. Concepts of sensitivity are used to determine variations of response to changes in parameter values for specific network realizations and as a basis for optimization in computer-aided design. Also included are several chapters describing the representation of linear networks as multi-terminal and multi-port networks. A solutions manual is available.

Price U.S. $62.95   Canada $72.95
0-916460-10-X, 648 pp./335 illus. 6" x 9" hardcover

Fundamentals of Gas Dynamics
by Robert D. Zucker

Written for the undergraduate, this book requires a minimum of prerequisites. The approach is to develop all basic relations on a rigorous basis with equations that are valid for the general case of unsteady, three-dimensional flow of an arbitrary fluid. These relations are then simplified to approach meaningful engineering problems in one- and two-dimensional flow. All basic internal and external flows are covered with practical applications interwoven in the text. Examples and problems are provided in both the English and SI systems of units. Dr. Zucker is a professor in the department of aeronautics at the Naval Postgraduate School. A solutions manual is available.

Price U.S. $52.95   Canada $64.95
0-916460-12-6, 443 pp., 6" x 9" hardcover

About The Tutor Series

The Tutor Series is designed for the student who is experiencing difficulty with his coursework. The depth of discussion of topics is much greater in a Tutor Series book than that found in a typical textbook. Step-by-step explanations are provided in Tutor Series books along with examples, illustrations and solved problems to assist the student who is experiencing difficulty in mastering his coursework.

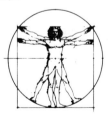

Digital Circuits: Engineer's Tutor Series
Volume 1: Numbering Systems, Binary Codes, Logic Gates, Boolean Algebra
by Amalou Abdelilah

Numerous examples help the student master the subject matter presented in this book. For example, in the section on binary codes, 8421 BCD is first discussed in a general sense. Six examples then follow which illustrate conversion between BCD and decimal. A step-by-step explanation is provided with each example so the reader fully understands the 8421 BCD/decimal conversion process.

Actual design experiments are also provided, complete with illustrations, wiring diagrams, and parts lists, to assist the student in his lab work. With its detailed explanations, many examples, solved problems and design experiments, *Digital Circuits: Engineer's Tutor Series* is an invaluable study aid for the engineering student who wishes to excel in his digital coursework.

Price U.S. $12.95   Canada $15.95
0-938862-67-7, 150 pp., 8½" x 11"

Digital Circuits: Engineer's Tutor Series
Volume 2: Truth Tables, Minterms, Maxterms, Karnaugh Maps
by Amalou Abdelilah

Price U.S. $12.95   Canada $15.95
0-929704-04-5, 120 pp., 8½" x 11"

Digital Circuits: Engineer's Tutor Series
Volume 3: Flip-Flops, Counters, Shift Registers, Decoders, Multiplexers
by Amalou Abdelilah

Price U.S. $12.95   Canada $15.95
0-929704-05-3, 220 pp., 8½" x 11"

Computer Books from Weber Systems, Inc.

IBM PC AT User's Handbook
by Weber Systems, Inc. Staff

The *IBM PC AT User's Handbook* is a complete guide to the IBM Personal Computer AT. This book is written in a clear, concise manner that allows a "first time" user to operate and program the Personal Computer AT. Although the book covers introductory concepts in depth, it also contains a great deal of information that is of interest to the experienced computer user.

The following topics are covered in detail in the *IBM PC AT User's Handbook*: installation, DOS, BASIC, error messages, debugging, and troubleshooting.

Numerous examples and illustrations are provided throughout the book.

Price U.S. $23.95   Canada $27.95
0-938862-06-5, 350 pp., 6" x 9"

The HP LaserJet Series II Printer
by Nathan Goldenthal

Written for the novice and advanced user alike, this book provides a thorough, comprehensive approach to the HP LaserJet Series II printer.

This book begins with fundamental concepts such as printer installation and operation. You will learn how to enter the printer settings from the front panel display.

The book continues with a detailed discussion of the PCL command language. The PCL commands are introduced and detailed in several chapters. Programming tips and techniques are also presented.

The book concludes with a discussion on software packages such as 1-2-3, dBASE and WordPerfect.

Price U.S. $24.95   Canada $29.95
0-938862-62-6, 375 pp., 7" x 10"

WordPerfect
Including the QuickStart Tutorial
by Jean Knox

This book is designed for the reader who wishes to learn to utilize WordPerfect efficiently while taking as little time as possible mastering the system. This book begins with *Section 1: The QuickStart Tutorial* which is designed to teach the reader basic Word-Perfect functions such as data entry, editing, file operation and printing in three hours or less. *Section 2: Advanced Topics and Tips* provides details on WordPerfect features such as macros, graphics, spreadsheet usage, special printer effects, and importing data. *Section 3: Applications* consists of individual examples which demonstrate how to undertake specific, practical tasks using WordPerfect such as financial reports, form letters, and term papers.

Price U.S. $24.95   Canada $29.95
0-938862-73-1, 500 pp., 7" x 10"

WordPerfect Simplified
by Jean Knox

WordPerfect is a powerful office and personal word processing tool. Like any other powerful tool, WordPerfect is complex. The purpose of *WordPerfect Simplified* is to clarify WordPerfect. Designed for the secretary, student or beginning computer user, this book will teach its readers how to enter, edit, save, and print a single or multi-page document.

WordPerfect Simplified includes numerous practical examples. The reader can quickly master WordPerfect by simply following each example on his computer. *WordPerfect Simplified's* hands-on, step-by-step approach makes this book ideal for anyone who wishes to master Word-Perfect quickly and efficiently.

Price U.S. $19.95   Canada $24.95
0-929704-01-1, 250 pp., 7" x 10"

DOS in a Day
by Jeff Weber

Even though MS-DOS is the most widely used personal computer operating system, many beginning DOS users find it cumbersome and difficult to learn. By presenting DOS in a simple, logical manner, *DOS in a Day* will teach you the fundamentals of DOS versions 3 or 4 in eight hours or less.

DOS in a Day takes a unique approach in its presentation of DOS. This book is divided into eight individual lessons, each of which is designed to be completed in less than one hour. Each lesson is designed around practice exercises which the reader actually undertakes on his computer. As the reader completes the practice exercises, he will add to his working knowledge of DOS.

Price U.S. $19.95   Canada $24.95
0-929704-14-2, 300 pp., 7" x 10"

MS-DOS: A Workbook
by Jeff Weber

MS-DOS: A Workbook takes a unique approach in its presentation of DOS. The purpose of this book is to present DOS topics one by one in an orderly, progressive manner so the reader is not overwhelmed, as is often the case, by a wealth of information all at once.

To accomplish this goal, this book is divided into 30 individual lessons, each of which is designed to be completed in less than one hour. Each lesson builds on the previous one so the reader continually expands his knowledge of DOS.

With its original modular design and hands-on approach, utilizing practice exercises, *MS-DOS: A Workbook* offers an ideal means for the prospective DOS user to master this subject.

Price U.S. $24.95   Canada $29.95
0-929704-15-0, 500 pp., 7" x 10"

These other Weber Systems titles may be ordered directly from the publisher at:

Weber Systems Inc.
8437 Mayfield Road
Chesterland, OH   44026
Phone: (216) 729-2858   FAX: (216) 729-3203

Please add a shipping and handling charge of $2.50 per item. Ohio residents should include 6.5% sales tax.